THE NOBLEST GAME

OXFORDSHIRE CRICKET CLUB.

ADMISSION TICKET SIGNED BY M. LAMBERT   A LATE
EIGHTEENTH-CENTURY ENGRAVING

THE
NOBLEST GAME

A BOOK OF
FINE CRICKET PRINTS

NEVILLE CARDUS *and* JOHN ARLOTT

HARRAP

London

ACKNOWLEDGMENTS

The Publishers would like to express their grateful appreciation to the following for permission to reproduce the plates in this book:

The Marylebone Cricket Club for Plates 1, 2, 3, 4, 6, 9, 11, 14, 16, 17, 18, 19, 20, 21, 22, 23, 24, 26, 27, 28, 29, 30, 31, 33, 35, 38, 39, 40, 41, 43, 44, 45, 46, 47, 49, 53, 54, 55, 56, 57, 58, 59, 63;
Mr John Arlott for Plates 5, 7, 8, 10, 13, 15, 32, 34, 36, 37, 42, 48, 50, 51, 52, 60, 61, 62, 64, for the frontispiece, and for the illustrations appearing on pages 15 and 21;
The La Trobe Collection, State Library of Victoria, for Plate 12;
Mr I. N. R. Shield for Plate 25.

The Publishers would also like to thank Mr Stephen Green, the Curator of the Marylebone Cricket Club, for the valuable assistance that he has rendered, and the Marylebone Cricket Club and Mr John Arlott for their co-operation and for generously granting photographic facilities.

First published in Great Britain 1969
by Harrap Limited
19-23 Ludgate Hill, London EC4M 7PD

Reissued 1986 with a new introduction
to cricket prints in history by John Arlott

© *Harrap Ltd 1986*

ISBN 0 245–54401–1

Designed by W. Bainbridge
Photography by P. Hirst-Smith
Research by R. Hawkins

Printed and bound in Great Britain
by Robert Hartnoll (1985) Ltd, Bodmin

PLATES

RICKET DISCOURSE

by Neville Cardus

IT is natural that man and boy, or girl if it comes to that, should play with a ball—
throw it, catch it, drive it with some propelling object, push it here and there, or roll
it by hand. Cleopatra, in a renowned moment, cried out "Lets to billiards." As far
back as 1560, some embryonic form of cricket was played; John Derrick, a Queen's
Coroner, writes that he and several other boys of the Free School of Guildford, "did
run and played there at crickett". The learned and lamented H. S. Altham, after
excavating this historic statement of John Derrick, expresses surprise in his and
E. W. Swanton's history that there is no explicit reference to cricket in Shakespeare;
but, if I remember well, Shakespeare (or one of his characters) describes somebody as
"a good bowler". And Shakespeare was prophetic enough to point out that some
other child of his imagination

> . . . . altogether lacks the abilities
> That Rhodes is dress'd in.

The game began in Kent, Sussex, Hampshire, and London. In the latter half of the
eighteenth century the aristocratically supported Hambledon club first established the
fundamental techniques of the game and, by the happy coincidence of John Nyren's
presence, was recorded in compelling prose. But before the Hambledon men marched
or ran into history, Kent cricketers claimed championship by beating "All England"
in June 1741, a victory which prompted a poem by a certain John Love, in which a
missed catch at the crisis is recorded by some eloquent doggerel:

> The erring ball, amazing to be told,
> Slipped through his outstretch'd hand and mock'd his hold.

We can be sure, human nature being consistently the same, that some spectator
watching that poor, fallible fieldsman, said, as men in the crowds at Lancashire and
Yorkshire matches would say (once on a time), as long-on waited, hands and arms
supplicatory, when a hit endomed the heavens, "'E'll miss it, 'e'll ruddy well miss it."
Bliss must it have been in those early, formative summers to be alive while, impercep-
tibly, a game of bat and ball evolved into a national appurtenance, a part of England's
way of life, inseparable from summer—rain or shine.

The old Hambledon men, in their tricorn hats and buckled shoes, may seem, in
this technological epoch of the 1960s, to have been merely primitive. As a fact,

they were the great pioneers, the Monteverdis and Caccinis of cricket's growth and potentiality of progress. The Hambledon men themselves were a consequence of long, anonymous years of crude yokel activity in country fields, where a missile resembling a ball was thumped by a lusty yeoman wielding a rudely curved wooden implement, against a bowler aiming at a gate serving as wicket. In fact, early recorded cricket matches had a wicket resembling a small gate—two stumps of about twenty-two inches tall, holding a bail six inches wide; no middle stump. The ''laws'' of cricket have usually been formulated not by abstract reasoning but pragmatically, from experience actual and illuminating. Five of Hambledon, one day, coping with five of All England, needed fourteen for victory when the last Hambledon batsman came to the crease, none other than John Small (of whom more anon). ''Lumpy'' Stevens many times got the ball past Small's bat, only to see it skid harmlessly between the two stumps. Hambledon won this match, but out of a bowler's frustration, out of justice to the straightness of his aim, a middle stump was later added and rendered legally accessory.

Today the mistake is often made of framing or amending cricket's laws by abstract reasoning, or by *a priori* argument, which is misguided, because abstract reasoning is not usually one of a professional cricketer's (which term now includes amateurs or ''Gentlemen'') basic mental powers. From the game's cradle, onward to the coming of W. G. Grace (the Bach of cricket) necessity was the mother of legal invention, as we shall see when we examine the first codified rules, published in 1744. I have seldom known these rules reproduced; I herewith extract them from a short review of cricket's history, in a book published by Longmans, Green and Co., more than thirty-eight years ago, written by myself. To this forgotten publication, and to its author, I am indebted for much information and research contained in the present essay of introduction. Here, then, are the first ''Laws of cricket'':

Laws for Ye Bowlers 4 Balls and Over

Ye Bowler must deliver ye Ball with one foot behind ye Crease even with ye Wicket, and when he has bowled one ball or more shall bowl to ye number 4 before he changes Wickets, and he shall change but once in ye same Innings.

He may order ye Player that is in at his Wicket to stand on which side of it he pleases at a reasonable distance.

If he delivers ye Ball with his hinder foot over ye bowling Crease, ye Umpire shall call No Ball, though she be struck, or ye Player is bowled out, which he shall do without being asked, and no Person shall have any right to ask him.

Laws for ye Strikers, or those that are in

If ye Wicket is Bowled down, its Out.

If he strikes, or treads down, or falls himself upon ye Wicket in striking, but not in over running, its Out.

A stroke or nip over or under his Batt, or upon his hands, but not arms, if ye Ball be held before she touches ye ground, though she be hug'd to the body, its Out.

If in striking both his feet are over ye popping Crease and his Wicket put down, except his Batt is down within, its Out.

If he runs out of his Ground to hinder a catch, its Out.

If a ball is nipp'd up and he strikes her again, wilfully, before she comes to ye Wicket, its Out.

If ye Players have cross'd each other, he that runs for ye Wicket that is put down is Out. If they are not cross'd he that returns is Out.

Batt Foot or Hand over ye Crease

If in running a notch ye Wicket is struck down by a throw, before his foot hand or Batt is over ye popping Crease, or a stump hit by ye Ball though ye Bail was down, its Out. But if ye Bail is down before, he that catches ye Ball must strike a Stump out of ye ground, Ball in hand, then its Out.

If ye Striker touches or takes up ye Ball before she is lain quite still unless asked by ye Bowler or Wicket-keeper, its Out.

When ye Ball has been in hand by one of ye Keepers or Stopers, and ye Player has been at home, He may go where he pleases till ye next ball is bowled.

If either of ye Strikers is cross'd in his running ground designedly, which design must be determined by the Umpires, N.B. The Umpire(s) may order that Notch to be scored.

When ye Ball is hit up, either of ye Strikers may hinder ye catch in his running ground, or if she's hit directly across ye wickets, ye other Player may place his body anywhere within ye swing of his Batt, so as to hinder ye Bowler from catching her, but he must neither strike at her nor touch her with his hands.

If a Striker nips a ball up just before him, he may fall before his Wicket, or pop down his Batt before she comes to it, to save it.

Ye Bail hanging on one Stump, though ye Ball hit ye Wicket, its Not Out.

Laws for Wicket Keepers

Ye Wicket Keepers shall stand at a reasonable distance behind ye Wicket, and shall not move till ye Ball is out of ye Bowlers hand, and shall not by any noise incommode ye Striker, and if his hands knees foot or head be over or before ye Wicket, though ye Ball hit it, it shall not be Out.

Laws for ye Umpires

To allow 2 Minutes for each Man to come in when one is out, and 10 minutes between each Hand.

To mark ye Ball that it may not be changed.

They are sole judges of all Outs and Ins, of all fair and unfair play, of frivolous delays, of all hurts, whether real or pretended, and are discretionally to allow what time they think proper before ye Game goes on again.

In case of a real hurt to a Striker, they are to allow another to come in and ye Person hurt to come in again, but are not to allow a fresh Man to play, on either Side, on any Account.

They are sole judges of all hindrances, crossing ye Players in running, and standing unfair to strike, and in case of hindrance may order a Notch to be scored.

They are not to order any Man out unless appealed to by any one of ye Players.

(These Laws are to ye Umpires Jointly.)

Each Umpire is sole judge of all Nips and Catches, Ins and Outs, good or bad Runs, at his own Wicket, and his determination shall be absolute, and he shall not be changed for another Umpire without ye consent of both Sides.

When 4 Balls are bowled, he is to call Over.

(These Laws are Separately.)

When both Umpires shall call Play, 3 times, 'tis at ye peril of giving ye Game from them that refuse to Play.

The observant student, considering the above first written Constitution of cricket, will note that there is no reference to leg-before-wicket. Maybe the game was all the better for lack of this rule. In "modern" first-class matches, often the batsman's main concern is to "get round" the "l.b.w." commandment; but C. B. Fry once asserted to me that in his period he and other Mandarins of the so-called "Golden Age" never dreamt of using deliberately their padded legs as a "first line of defence"—"an affront to aesthetic morality", maintained Fry. I wonder what Freddie Trueman would have said, had he appealed for "l.b.w." and been told by the umpire to remember his "aesthetic morality".

One of the 1744 rules, it will be noted, says "Ye Bail hanging on one Stump, though ye Ball hit ye Wicket, its Not Out"—another instruction in the Tablature which has provoked in bowlers mortification and sense of the world's injustice, to this day. Not many years ago, Yorkshire were playing Cambridge University, at Fenner's. A ball from Macaulay beat a university batsman's groping forward lunge and hit the middle stump. Marvellously the bails remained intact. The whole of the Yorkshire XI crowded around the wicket, consternated and voluble about this phenomenon of dynamics. The bails were blown at by the strong breath of Yorkshire's wicket-keeper, Arthur Wood. Nothing, of course, could be done about it; the Cambridge batsman was "Not Out". The umpires ordered the Yorkshire XI back to their several fielding positions, to which they proceeded still voluble, if fortunately not widely heard. But, as Macaulay was about to bowl the next ball, Arthur Wood, from behind the outraging stumps, leant forward and asked the lucky-starred batsman: "Excuse me, but has thi tried walkin' on water?" ("Water" pronounced to rhyme with "martyr").

A certain other procedure of the Hambledonians has been perpetuated to the present time, though subtly and geologically transformed. Bowlers in that distant era had the privilege of selecting the playing pitch. "Lumpy" Stevens invariable chose "the brow of the hill", so that his best "shooter" would receive from the pitch some added velocity. It is the groundsman, today, who likewise "selects" the playing pitch, preparing it in such a way that the "home" XI's attack is more or less "accommodated" (as Corporal Pistol would put it). When Surrey CCC won the County Championship seven consecutive times, between 1952 and 1958, it was not only Tony but Bert Lock (Bert Lock, of course, was then the groundsman of Kennington Oval) who led the way to these repeated triumphs and conquests.

I must certainly—for humour's sake—tell of two other examples of pragmatical law-making in cricket, of procedure and change of rule governed by bitter experience. At the beginning of the eighteenth century, a hole was dug, or rounded, at the centre

of the two-stump wicket. The batsman was required to ground his bat into the hole to score his runs. To run him out, the fieldsman was required to place the ball into the hole before the batsman got there. It began to happen too frequently that the fieldsman's hand and the batsman's bat arrived in the hole simultaneously. Hence adjustment again; to quote the proper legal terminology, "adherence to precedent, coupled with a power of modifying precedent to circumstance".

The Hambledonians, as every historian of cricket knows, bowled with an under-arm action, much as the gentleman in *Pickwick*, who gripped the ball, closed one eye to focus aim, then cried out, in a fierce voice, "Play!" John Nyren, chronicler of Hambledon cricket, described Harris's action this way: "He would bring the ball from under the arm by a twist, and nearly as high as his arm-pit, and with this action *push* it, as it were, from him." The "scientific" exploiter of seam and "shine" of today may well smile patronizingly at the notion of a "lob" or under-arm bowler trying to cope with, say, Boycott or Lawry, or any master batsman of our decade of sophistication. These doubters of the efficiency of the ball delivered under-arm might reflect that against South African batsmen as "modern" and as gifted as any presently on view, Simpson-Hayward took twenty-three wickets for England in the Test Matches of 1909–10, played in South Africa. His victims included one of the greatest batsmen ever, Aubrey Faulkner, also Commaile, J. H. Sinclair (a fearsome striker of the ball), A. D. Nourse (as canny and as hard to overthrow as Lawry himself), and Gordon White (equal as batsman to, say, D'Oliviera).

My other instance of invention, and the Comic Spirit governing legality in cricket, emerged from the omission in the 1744 Laws of any clause restricting the width of bat, which, as we have been authoritatively informed, then resembled a hockey stick, rather more "clubbed". One summer day, in a game at Reigate, a batsman took guard with a bat wider than the wicket, completely obscuring sight of the stumps, a blade rendering him, did he decide never to lift it from the ground, invincible,

15

impenetrable. Thus, yet again, amendment of procedure by force of pressure of experience.

John Small, born in 1737, once held the "All-England" bowlers at bay for three days. It is incredibly recorded that he was not "clean bowled" for several years. He was known by men of Hambledon chiefly as a "defensive" player; also he was musical, with the "tenor violin". He made the implements of cricket, hanging from his shop a painted sign declaring:

> Here lives John Small
> Makes Bat and Ball
> Pitch a Wicket, Play at Cricket
> With any Man in England.

The Hambledon and Kent men truly created the "Noble and Elegant Game". Primitives? As out of modern fashion and vision as tall hats? The fact is that they inspired some of the game's lasting literature by Nyren, Pycroft, and Mitford. There were Masters then and characters to write about. "It was a study", wrote Mitford, "for Phidias, to see Beldham rise to strike; the grandeur of the attitude, the settled composure of the look, the piercing lightning of the eye, the rapid glance of the bat . . ." Nyren, Beldham, Brett, Small, Harris, Sueter, Stevens, Walker, not to forget Pilch and Mynn—they are safe for posterity in the game's Parthenon.

The antique engravings, depicting cricket matches usually set in a Constable landscape, often show the umpires holding a bat. I have never understood why. Was the bat used by the umpires of old as shooting-sticks to rest themselves on; or were they there, close at hand, in case some mighty clouter of the ball broke his bat? As I dwell upon this question, I am reminded of Augustine Birrell's first and only appearance at the wicket. He was a politician and a man of letters—Victorian and early Edwardian. J. M. Barrie persuaded him to take part in a game at Stanway in Gloucestershire, where Barrie many a summer gathered together cricket XIs of strangely mixed performers. Birrell went forth to the wicket using a borrowed bat. Attempting a huge on-drive, eyes tightly closed, he split the bat in twain. Not in the least disconcerted, he waved to the pavilion with the broken pieces of willow, crying out, "Bring me some more bats."

As soon as the Hambledon, Sussex, and Kent men sent their under-arm bowling curving through the air, and not skidding along the ground, obviously the hockey-curved bat could no longer serve, either as defensive or offensive weapon. Hence the advent of the straight-shouldered blade; and one of its first salesmen, even if he didn't evolve it from his inner consciousness, was a certain White of Reigate, round about 1773. As we have related, to our general enjoyment, nothing was stipulated in law restricting the width of the blade until 1774.

The progress from under-arm to round-arm bowling was inevitable. Every boy throws a ball, or any stone he picks up, as instinctively as he runs or leaps. I imagine the first bowling aimed at the batsman from shoulder level occurred because of sheer vexation on the bowler's part. Batsmen became quick of foot. One, named John Hammond, ran out of his crease to a "lob" from the stately Lord Frederick Beauclerk and nearly decapitated him. Tom Walker was "no-balled" for throwing some two decades before John Willes of Maidstone, or thereabouts, "got away" with it; but it needed years to convince the Establishment of the "fairness" of this method. Willes was "no-balled" at Lord's, playing for Kent v. MCC. He disgustedly jumped on his horse and departed. Round-arm bowling has actually been seen in first-class cricket by lovers of the game still in the prime of life. Clarrie Grimmett, subtlest of Australian leg-spinners and "googlists" (circa 1926–37), released his floating, revolving trickery from an arm elevated not much above shoulder level. So did E. R. ("Rockley") Wilson, Yorkshire and England, in the early 1920s. Wilson was a scholar and master at Winchester, an encyclopaedic cricketologist also. His devotion to cricket and to the greatest of cricketers was such that, in his house at Winchester, he signified the whereabouts of the toilet in bold ornamental letters—"W.G."

Not until 1864 was over-arm bowling sanctioned, though clearly the transition from round-arm to over-arm was an inevitable advance. The famous William Lilly-white, according to Altham, raised his arm above the shoulder as far back as 1827. The march of progress, as Edmund Burke maintained, is slow. Alfred Mynn, as legendary and as select amongst Kent cricketers as Woolley himself, exploited the round-arm attack from round the wicket, causing the ball to "leave" the bat danger-ously. Was he, without knowing it, father of the "Barnes" ball, the incomparable Sidney Barnes's master-trick? Amongst other round-arm bowlers of our own, or recently our own, period must be counted the aforementioned J. M. Barrie, known also as a playwright of yester-year. He bowled round-arm at so slow a pace that, he claimed, if he didn't like the look of the ball he had delivered, he could (quote) "run after it and bring it back" (end of quote).

As this introduction is not a history, I can merely mention the names of the great Hambledon, Sussex, and Kentish players who ploughed and sowed the soil out of which was to come the game's full and "modern" burgeonings: "Silver Billy" Beldham, Pilch, Wisden, Lambert, Clarke, Walker, Small, Harris, Lillywhite, "Felix", Wenman, and Alfred Mynn, to name a few immortals. I can't trace the name of the genius who first bowled over-arm—round about 1860, setting a fashion before which the Law had at last to submit. I suspect that Alfred Mynn, pupil as a bowler of the revolutionary Willes, more often than not raised his arm above shoulder. He was six feet high and weighed eighteen stones. "With a few deliberate and majestic strides," writes Altham, "bringing his arm round in a swing as smooth as a piston-rod, he projected the ball assuredly faster than any English bowler of today"—a tall statement to make in 1926. A more or less historically anonymous Brown of Brighton was reputed to have released the ball at so great a speed as to kill a dog on the boundary behind the wicket. Lillywhite, we may justly assume, was not above raising his arm higher than the statutory position or plane of his epoch. He was artful enough, so were a number of these ancient manipulators of Bat and Ball. Seen through the enchanting mists of years, and by reason of the way they are so picturesquely presented in the prints, they seem to have lived and played in a glow of elegance and "nobility". Fortunately for the embracing spirit of cricket, humour collaborated with "manliness"; Tom Lockyer, wicket-keeper for Surrey, hinted to an innocent, trusting batsman that he would be wise to pat down some uneven spot on the pitch. When the batsman moved out of his crease to do so, Lockyer swept off the bails.

The nineteenth century tended to endow cricket with associations ethical and exemplary. "It's not cricket." "A straight bat and a modest mind." Such was the cant. May I again temporarily bring out of the limbo the short Longmans history referred to above and quote? "This perpetual insistence on the 'gentlemanliness' of cricket seems to me as unnecessary as it is offensive. . . .Why, when footballers and jockeys 'play the game', are *they* not the subject of moral approbation?" The truth is that the Hambledonians, the Kentish men, and their contemporaries, were usually men of juiciness and shrewdness. Some of them accepted a fee to do their best, not only to win, but to lose. Betting became rampant. Nowadays first-class cricket is so long-drawn-out that it is a poor incitement to the instincts of a true (and necessarily impatient) gambler. Single-wicket matches, one player pitted against another, were in vogue long ago. We are today seeing cricket coming full circle; one-day contests for the Gillette Cup, one renowned master versus another, and betting! Some of our first-class county pitches also suggest a return to nature, because of their capacity to aid and abet a "shooter" and a "bouncer".

When over-arm bowling was legalized in the early 1860s, the stage was ready for cricket as we know it now. Moreover, with the advent of industry and factories and coalmines in the Midlands and North of England, the game spread in activity from the agricultural South. "Cometh the hour, cometh the man." Genius is not a mushroom growth; genius sums up periods of sowing, periods of progress by trial and error, periods of empiricism. Goethe argued that it could make all the difference to a genius if he were born ten years earlier or ten years later. W. G. Grace was fifteen years old when, in 1863, he scored thirty-two against an All-England XI. Over-arm bowling was then a fairly new trick of the bowler's trade. Grace mastered the first rude practitioners of slinging pace. In the late summer of his life, his "Jubilee", he took the lightning attack of C. J. Kortright by the scruff of the neck, scoring a century—and Kortright was as "modern" and as fast as Statham, Trueman, and West Indies' Hall, to say the least. Kortright, to his life's end, never ceased to extol "W. G.", who waited for the bowling with the toe of his left foot confidently raised. In a match between Essex and some county or other, a young university batsman came to the wicket, took guard, then stood with his toe cocked up, like the "Old Man". "I was about to bowl," narrated Kortright, "so I said to him, 'Put your toe down; I allow nobody except "W. G." to face me with his toe up.' But the young cove declined to put his toe down, which was an impertinence to me. I sent him a 'yorker' bang on that same cocked-up toe, and he had to be carried back to the pavilion."

"W. G." was undoubtedly the Father of cricket as, at the present time, it is organized and understood. He slaughtered the fast bowling of his earlier years. Multitudes of spectators paid to see him everywhere. He provided much of the financial needs of the new-born county teams. From 1879 until 1908, he dominated the game, his beard as Institutional as Mr Gladstone's collar. He was Johnsonian, imposing of build and by word of mouth. It is generally forgotten, though, that as a young man Grace was athletic; he could throw a cricket ball 118 yards, and run like the wind. But he is enshrined in the Permanent National Portrait Gallery of Cricket as the nation recognized him in 1895, when, in May, in his forty-seventh year, he amassed a thousand runs. In his career he scored 54,896 runs, average nearly 40, and took 2876 wickets, by means of slow suggestions of leg-breaks, supported by his overwhelming personal and vocal authority. Umpires stood in awe of him. In a high voice he would appeal "How's that?" It was really a dogmatic personal verdict. Still, of those 2876 wickets taken by "W. G." in his countless days in the sun, *some* of them must have really been "out".

A. E. Lawton, once amateur player for Derbyshire, told me of an experience he enjoyed with "W. G." He was young and fresh to first-class cricket. When he went in to bat, "W. G." was wheeling up his slow, high-tossed bowling, with a fieldsman stationed at deep long-leg. "W. G.'s" idea was to tempt the batsman to send a catch clean into deep long-leg's hands. But Lawton declined to swallow the bait; he merely pushed "W. G.'s" "donkey drops" for singles to the on-side. After a few overs, "W. G." stopped his run to bowl and called down the pitch to Lawton: "See you here, young feller—if you keep on playing my bowling this way I'll take myself off, I will—I'll take myself off!" All said in a high voice.

I can never cease to marvel over the fact that in 1871 "W. G." scored 2739 runs, average 78·90, and that the next most prolific run-maker of this summer of 1871 was Richard Daft, average 37. Nowadays there is no such statistical discrepancy to mark the difference in skill and productivity (blessed word) between one eminent batsman and another. Moreover, in 1871, "W. G." was obliged to cope with appallingly uncertain pitches, especially at Lord's. He was cheered by the onlookers when he got his bat down to four consecutive "shooters", balls of pace, which skidded like a stone thrown over an icy surface. "W. G.'s" mastery against fast bowling had an influence on all sorts of bowling, though, of course, spin, flight, and variation of speed were becoming more and more subtilized, as a consequence of a natural development of methods inherited. "W. G.'s" great contribution to the technique of cricket was a synthesis of nearly all the principles of batsmanship established by his forerunners, accumulated by time and experiment, since the cricketers of Hambledon, Kent, and Sussex changed "Bat and Ball" into the "Noblest" (and the most comprehensively skilful) of games, calling for a variety of skills, different methods of bowling, different methods of batsmanship. "W. G.", to use a musical metaphor, took the themes invented by predecessors and elaborated them into a large-spanned symphony, a symphony not only of cricket, but one which could express English character, reflect the summer's changes of light and shade, and relate itself to an environment. Yorkshire cricket has always had a different aspect, a different accent and approach, from Kent cricket. Wilfred Rhodes could scarcely have emanated from Lord's or Brighton. He and George Hirst, and David Denton, Haigh, Emmott Robinson, George Macaulay, right down to Brian Close and Freddie Trueman, have played the game in Yorkshire language, played it with Yorkshire relish. Woolley's cricket remained, from his first of all innings to his last, faithful to Kent; I can see it, in memory, as perpetually set against a background of Canterbury, Maidstone, Tunbridge.

The nineteenth century was individual, not, as today, a period in which all men are equal, some more equal than others. I have for years maintained that cricket is responsive, more than any other game, to environment, to the soil and atmosphere in which it is cradled and has grown up. At the present time the general uniformity of cricketers, the shortage of "character", of immediately recognizable personal identity, is an effect of the levelling, or equalizing, of life in a technological age. The style in cricket was once the man himself. Even a player from the West Indies is becoming standardized, Anglicized, or Australianized, in method and technical aspect. I could, put to it, relate Sobers (much to his credit) to Woolley. Lord Learie Constantine was West Indies cricket *in excelsis*, instinctive, impulsive, racial, charged with animal spirits. I love to tell (and to repeat) of an afternoon at Lord's in 1928. Middlesex v. the West Indies began a second innings 122 runs ahead. Constantine ran amok. (He was, so Sir Jack Hobbs asserted, the fastest bowler that he, the Master of them all, ever faced—for half a dozen overs or so.) Constantine destroyed Middlesex's second innings; he swept seven batsmen out of his way for 57, stumps flying and splitting. Then he cut, hooked, and drove 103 runs out of 133, in an hour, achieving for the West Indies a miraculous victory. Watching this match was a visitor from the West Indies, obviously at Lord's for the first time, so he had dressed, as he thought, appropriately—grey frock coat, striped trousers, a tie of many colours. He watched from near the Pavilion the West Indies collapse earlier on; but at the blazing crescendo in Constantine's innings, he projected himself from his seat amongst the *élite* of Lord's and, in shining black shoes, adorned with white spats, he ran round the boundary to the stand at the Nursery End, where hundreds of West Indian spectators were jubilating; he ran waving a rolled umbrella to his compatriots, crying out, "I'm coming to join you, boys—I'm coming to join you." He had been inspired by Constantine's West Indian genius to break free of the barriers imposed by fashion, class, frock coats, and spats.

The most remarkable instance of all of cricket's ability to manifest not only individuality but to contain and express race and breed was K. S. Ranjitsinhji. He came to cricket in this country at a moment when the game was as English as well could be: Victorian in deportment sometimes. The straight bat, the honest good-length ball, no obliquities of "googly" bowling, the "Noble" game as sanctioned by "W. G.", the MCC, Lord Harris, and Lord Hawke. Into English cricket "Ranji" brought a gleam from the Orient, his bat a wand of magical conjuration. The fast ball coming on to "Ranji's" middle stump was—against all Christian precedent—flicked round to leg. The fast bowler was aghast. I have made known for years "Ted" Wainwright's opinion of Ranjitsinhji's batting. Wainwright played for Yorkshire and for England. "Ranji," he expostulated, "why, he never made a Christian stroke in his life." Ranjitsinhji, in his high noon, was the most magnetic of all batsmen; for ease of mastery, sinuous grace, and fascination of aspect, none has surpassed him. Even the silk of his shirt appeared to flutter as though from the enchanting sensibility of his blood and his nerve and his swiftly subtle intelligence. In 1900, he scored (or invocated) no fewer than 3065 runs, average 87, including five double centuries, all for Sussex. His career record was 24,567 runs, average 45. For England, his runs amounted to 989, average 45. Two of his Test match innings have mingled with the legendary lore of the game: 154 not out v. Australia, at Manchester, 1896; and 175, at Sydney, for A. E. Stoddart's England XI of 1897–98. The irony of "Ranji's" fabulous summers is that in 1902 he stupendously failed against Australia, in this country, with a sequence of 13, 0, 2, and 0. All the world of cricket marvelled; all the world of cricket had taken the witchcraft of his batsmanship for granted. Maybe his most genius-informed innings was for Sussex v. Middlesex at Brighton. On a terrible pitch, against the spin of

PARKER'S PIECE, CAMBRIDGE 1854

Trott, Hearne, and Rawlin, he scored 202; nobody else except Vine (17) arrived at double figures. There was another "Ranji" miracle performed at Brighton, again for Sussex, this time v. Lancashire. C. B. Fry loved to tell the story. "On the closing day, Saturday"—matches then began on Mondays and Thursdays—"Sussex, playing Lancashire, were virtually beaten. 'Ranji' had strained his left wrist, and on the Friday evening, he said he would be unable to take further part in the game. The Lancashire XI were elated—they would be free early on Saturday afternoon to get back to Manchester. But on the Saturday morning 'Ranji' decided he might, at the pinch, be capable of defending his wicket one-handed. As a fact, he scored 200, saving Sussex from what had looked like certain defeat." Then Fry would take a breath and continue, "But although it is generally known by students of cricket that 'Ranji' on this occasion scored a double century on a fiery, broken pitch, while he was hindered by a useless left wrist, it is not as well known that also he was handicapped by another physical disability—*corns*!" Ranjitsinhji was an original cricketer, issuing from no forerunner, a wonder of spontaneous creation, translating, as I say, the "Noble" English game into realms of Oriental wizardry, loveliness, and strangely hidden power. His drives might have burnt the grass with their electrical current, but there was in his strokeplay no sign of muscular forcibility. He was a midsummer night's dream of cricket.

His necromancy has led me temporarily astray from proper historical sequence. The game spread from the green fields and meadows of Hampshire, Kent, and Sussex when

21

industry created the populous cities of the North and Midlands of England. The professional players emerged from places, like Nottingham especially, where time was available for cricket because of the system of work by handloom at home. William Attewell, accurate length bowler, in the line of succession of Alfred Shaw, also a Nottingham product, was senior at the nets at Shrewsbury School in 1912; and I was his assistant. He would talk of olden times, of his opportunity to make his living at the handloom of his cottage. He could work whenever he chose, often at night, after a day of cricket. In Yorkshire the same freedom to exercise one's craft or trade, though different in procedure and method, was prevalent. Consequently it was possible to play cricket on mid-week afternoons. So, gradually, the County Championship was evolved; but not until 1890 was there a division of first- and second-class teams. It is not generally known that as far back as 1839 Sussex was a county club playing matches at Brighton; and the historians have recorded that in 1873 Gloucestershire and Nottinghamshire achieved a "dead heat" as leaders in a county tourney. The advance became rapid. County engagements increased from some twenty odd in 1870 to fifty in 1880. And the roll of representative names, now part and parcel of cricket's Pantheon of immortal characters, and technical innovators, acquired traditional prestige and succession. Alfred Shaw was as seminal, as influential in method and tactics, as a bowler, as Grace was as a batsman. He bowled, in his career, nearly 25,000 overs: and of these four-ball overs no fewer than nearly 17,000 were maidens. Altogether his harvest of wickets, pitching the ball to a nicety, was 2051. He established the off-theory tactics which prevailed throughout the nineteenth century, the field crowded on the off-side. A ball pitched on the leg-side was a crude fall from grace. The bowler usually apologized to his captain, "Sorry, sir, it slipped!"

At Johannesburg, in January 1906, England lost a Test Match v. South Africa—South Africa's first defeat of England—by one wicket. The winning hit was made from a leg-side-pitched ball from Relf; and P. F. Warner, England's captain, cried out of his heart, "Oh, Albert, how could you?"

"Off-theory", an attack directed on or outside the off-stump, supported by a crowded off-side field, no doubt occasionally caused slow scoring, but it had a certain aesthetic or spectacular advantage over the present-day bowler's obsession—short of a length stuff in-swinging, with two leg-side fieldsmen behind the popping crease, there to pick up catches. (Until recently there was no limit to the amount of fieldsmen a bowler could place on the leg-side.) Off-theory did not cramp free and beautiful strokes, as in-swingers to leg do; moreover, off-theory naturally and logically called for brilliant *mobile* fielding at cover-point, mid-off, extra cover, and so on. Yet at the noon of the "Golden Age" of the 1890s and 1900s, there were slow scorers; Scotton, for example, who, in the Oval Test Match of 1886, England v. Australia, scored thirty-four in three and three-quarter hours. I remember old Attewell reminiscent, in 1912; I tried to "draw" him sentimentally by saying, "They don't hit the ball nowadays as hard as in your day." He denied this statement with some indignation. "They hit it harder," he vowed. "You young fellers don't know nothin' about stonewallin'. I once saw Scotton bat for an hour and a half. And do you know how many he made? He made none. That were stonewallin' for you!" He was obviously proud of Scotton's achievement; he obviously regarded Scotton as one of the heroes of the departed "Golden

Age''. When we attempt a comparison of batsmen's rate of scoring over the decades, it is as well to keep in mind that an over consisted of four balls from 1880 to 1888, and five from then onward until round about 1901–2. At Kennington Oval, in August 1882, Australia beat England for the first time in this country, as every schoolboy should know, if he knows what is a cricket bat at sight. The match was lost and won by seven runs; and at the crisis Spofforth bowled maiden after maiden, a change of field, every four balls. No wonder a spectator in the Pavilion chewed the curved top of his umbrella almost to liquidity.

In general the pace of scoring has remained much the same during the past half-century. But the manner of it all, the style and approach to the game, was less acquisitive, less cannily protective, than has happened most times in cricket in the decade beginning 1955, or thereabouts. The most important factor in the period extending from Grace's dominance to the era of MacLaren, ''Ranji'', Jessop, C. B. Fry, F. S. Jackson, and P. F. Warner, to mention a few names, was the ''amateur'' example. What's bred in the bone will come out in the shortest innings. Men of the independent minds (not necessarily of independent means!) such as MacLaren, Fry, Jessop, and especially ''Ranji'', would not have chosen to spend sunny afternoons fielding for hours to the congested leg-pushes of—well, never mind. They would have gone, each and severally, to Ascot.

The contribution of public school and university to the full orchestration of cricket was immense, as the game entered its first ''Golden Age'', between, say, the 1880s to 1914. (The second ''Golden Age'' came to consummation in the 1930s.) From Grace to Hobbs, then from Hobbs to Sutcliffe, Hammond, and Compton; from Trumper to Macartney, from Macartney to Bradman. Circling round the main planets of each period were A. G. Steel, Spofforth, Shrewsbury, Giffen, Read, Lohmann, Stoddart, Briggs, MacLaren, William Gunn, Tyldesley, Hirst, Rhodes, C. B. Fry, F. S. Jackson, R. E. Foster, Noble, Jessop, P. F. Warner, Lockwood, and Richardson— and on and on, illustrious name after name, to the ''Master'' Hobbs, and George Gunn, S. F. Barnes, Woolley, Gregory, Tate, Macdonald, Larwood, culminating in the great renaissance crowned by Hutton, Compton, Bradman, Lindwall, Harvey, and Miller. But it is invidious to pick out names: it is shorthand historical summary to leave out South African artists of the calibre of H. W. Taylor, the Nourses. And there was another conjuror of the bat from India—Duleepsinhji. The amateur, as he was once on a time called, usually provided the backbone, and the style, of England's batsmanship. In 1900, there were fourteen amateurs in the season's first twenty-one leading batsmen, and seven professionals. In this same summer of 1900, Ranjitsinhji and Fry between them amassed 5390 runs, with a joint average of 73. (In 1947 Compton and Edrich between them amassed no fewer than 7355, averaging 85.) In 1901, C. B. Fry staggered cricket credulity by scoring six centuries in consecutive innings. Even Grace, Trumper, and ''Ranji'' had not performed such a marvel of persistent, acquisitive batsmanship. Thirty-seven years later the same achievement, six successive hundreds, was rendered easy as gathering fruit by Bradman.

From the 1880s, until the end of the Edwardian epoch, first-class cricket more or less reflected the social setting and structure of this country at large. Gentlemen v. Players. The amateurs went into the field, and came back from it, through the main

23

Pavilion entrance; the professionals used another and smaller gate, a sort of "servants' entrance". No professional of the 1900s would have dreamt of addressing A. C. MacLaren as "Archie". Yet there was no servility about, say, J. T. Tyldesley, when he said "Sir" to MacLaren. The professionals took their cue from the amateurs and much of their way of approach to the game. "You couldn't", so J. T. Tydesley explained to me, "play dull or crude cricket with Mr Spooner or Mr MacLaren batting at the other end." The first-class game, the County Championship, throve on the subscriptions of the county gentry. The *hoi polloi*, I sometimes suspected when I was one of them, were not really welcomed at the large enclosures—admission (to the "working classes") 6d. "No money returned," was the warning sign: "You enter at your own risk." Matches, even Test Matches in England, limited to three days, began on Mondays or Thursdays. Frequently the vast spaces of Lord's, the Oval, Headingley, and Trent Bridge would be vacant on Saturdays, the match having been finished on Friday, or before lunch on Saturday. The fine arts of groundsmanship produced, in dry weather, firm, fast turf, which after sun and rain turned into vicious collaborators with spin bowlers. In 1902, in an English season of pitches spitting venom, bowlers' paradises, Victor Trumper scored eleven centuries and 2570 runs, average 48·49, against Rhodes, Blythe, Wass (fast from leg to off-stump), Mead, Barnes, J. T. Hearne, and others skilled in twisting devilry with the ball. In the 1890s, to the advent of "Ranji", Trumper, MacLaren, Fry, Hayward, and the first "Golden Age" vintage cricketers, there were fast bowlers in abundance, spinners left arm and right, slow and medium; but the leg-break remained a curiosity, rather suspect, until Leonard Braund, D. W. Carr, and Bosanquet, the first "googly" practitioner, came on the scene. Also the "seamer", so familiar and obsessive today in the later 1960s, had little scope, for the simple reason that until round about 1910, only one and the same ball was legally available during the batting-side's innings. As Jack Gunn, brother of the unique George, once put it to me: "We had to mek do with same ball, till it come in two—then we were allowed an old ball in its place." Tom Richardson, fast bowler for Surrey and England, took 1005 wickets, in four seasons—1894–97—at 14 runs each, using most times a ball shorn of "shine" and seam. What is more, he needed to slave and sweat, bowling on pluperfect wickets at Kennington Oval. Ranjitsinhji maintained that Lockwood was a more dangerous fast bowler than Richardson; but Lockwood himself, in his old age, declared that "compared with Richardson, he was not in the same parish".

So the game and its implements, its material, social and peopled environment, have been changed, time after time, responsive to the influences of scene and circumstances. As I have suggested, first-class cricket seems nowadays to be returning partly to conditions of its nonage—one-day matches and pitches uncertain of behaviour, unfriendly to batsmen, pitches likely to have been chosen by the prehistoric Hambledon, Kent, and Sussex men. But never again shall we watch cricket set against a background of green trees, haystacks, barns, and a landscape of peace and plenty, remote from a world too busy getting and spending. That is one reason why the prints in this book are jealously worth preserving, a refreshment to eye and mind, constantly renewing our love of "The Noble Game".

CRICKET PRINTS IN HISTORY

by John Arlott

THE introduction—called "Cricket Discourse"—to the first edition of this book was written by Sir Neville Cardus and it would be an o'erweening apprentice who assumed to supersede the master. Rather this should be seen as a tribute to Sir Neville and an echo of his outlook on the game. The delight of making, studying and enjoying the collection was mutual and this survivor can only hope that it is preserved in this following collection.

A collection of pictorial art of cricket is, in fact, important. Artists—especially, though, to a minor degree, the portrait artists—have over the years included sporting items—a dog, a horse saddle, a sword or a cricket bat—in their compositions incidentally, because sport is a part of British social life. The significance of this collection, though, is more serious. These are, with only the single exception of the portrait of Thomas Hope of Amsterdam (No. 22), purely cricket pictures. Their essence lies in the fact that although from 1750 to the present day the game of cricket has constantly changed overall vastly, yet it has always remained essentially the same, or in the words of Herbert Farjeon

The game that's done, the game
that's never done.

That has been so from the time when shepherd lads first played it on the South Downs to the time when it became the pursuit of the public schools and their progeny, and on to today. The first players of any stature were peasants of Kent, Sussex and Hampshire: many of them were hired by the Georgian and Regency gentry to play in matches for—relative to present-day standards—immense wagers.

The centres of great skill moved from the Weald to the northern Industrial Revolution powers of the Nottinghamshire, Lancashire and Yorkshire professionals. It partly withdrew to the amateurs of the "Golden Age" in the Edwardian period; and now is completely international—its centres no longer solely in Britain nor even Australia, but also in India, Pakistan, New Zealand, West Indies and Sri Lanka; and, to a lesser but not negligible extent, South Africa, East Africa, Hong Kong, Egypt, Malaysia, Denmark, Argentina, Holland, U.S.A., Canada, Fiji and Corfu.

The quality of pictures of most sports lies in their spectacularly athletic, or technical, significance. Cricket pictures, however, reflect an essential part of British life. No one would pretend that more people attend cricket than football matches. The largest cricket grounds barely hold 30,000 people, and that only for a few days a year. On the other hand, it does span all classes of society and virtually all ages since sport in England—as distinct from the blood sports—began. After its beginnings on the downs of the Weald, its next move was to the churchyards; many of the earliest written records of the game concern parishioners playing the game there on Sundays. Then it shifted the short distance to the village green where, despite its spread, it retains permanent roots, and has become part of the rural scene. If, though, it was a rural sport, it steadily became urban. Indeed, its most striking period of growth as a spectator sport was in the industrial North, coinciding largely with the introduction of the Saturday half-holiday, when enthusiasts happily stood on the terraces from two o'clock until half-past six, watching the play. Now, while it would be stupid to argue for it greater support than exists for Association Football, its following spreads across a wide swathe of the population. Moreover, to an extent that would be difficult to calculate, people throughout the country follow it through commentaries or the newspapers, even though many of them have rarely or never been to watch a first-class match in their lives. So, what these pictures depict is part of the life of the country; even the portraits manifestly come from all sections of the community.

The fact is that, once it has genuinely become part of life anywhere, cricket faithfully reflects the society in which it is played. Thus, it is plain from these pictures that the game and its background are different in Australia from the English form: not better nor worse, but different. It is different again in India and the West Indies; as will be apparent when it begins to produce art in those countries, apart from photography, which is a separate matter, certainly deserving a book—indeed, books—to itself.

Even at its most socially exalted pitch, cricket has always been a popular game. The broadsheet laws of the game were widely available; so were those outstanding manifestations of popular art, the lithographs of "Felix", and John Corbet Anderson, and G.F. Watts. Probably the widest and best example lay in cigarette cards; essentially, though, its art has never been restricted, but available to all who played or followed it. Certainly since the middle of the nineteenth century until almost the middle of the twentieth, pavilions, even the humblest of them, have had cricket pictures on their walls. For many years, even down to the nineteen-twenties, many of those buildings, though decaying structurally, carried some version of the huge 'National' print of a cricket match between the Counties of Sussex and Kent at Brighton, first published by W.H. Mason in 1849, and the joint effort of Mason, G.H. Phillips, W. Drummond and C.J. Basébe. It had, in the end, 72 figures of players and spectators, all to be identified on an outline provided with the original, but which is now far rarer than the original itself. This was probably the most popular of all cricket prints, even if the colour lithos of Anderson and his fellows were more distinguished.

Cricket cigarette cards had a rich period from about 1896 to 1936. Cricket photography probably reached two separate peaks; the first comprised the action photographs of G.W. Beldam (published in book form with accompanying text by C.B. Fry) of about 1905; and the work of Patrick Eagar in the 1980s.

Of all these plates the most historically significant and the most miraculous survival is the page from George Shepheard's sketchbook of 1790 (No. 2). It shows the first recorded giants of the game, those of Hambledon, as recorded in the first true literature of cricket—probably never bettered—by Richard Nyren. It is, of course, "The Cricketers of My Time", the second and major part of that author's *The Young Cricketer's Tutor* (1733), heightened by the retrospect of some fifty years; and probably helped by the editing of Charles Cowden Clarke.

Once any cricket enthusiast has read Nyren's book, Shepheard's drawings, amateurish as they may be, assume a new, and quite considerable, significance. The other high peak of cricket pictures was that attained by the caricaturists in the periodical *Vanity Fair,* which ran from 1868 to 1929. Many of the best of those on cricket subjects were by "Ape" (Carlo Pellegrini) and "Spy" (Sir Leslie Ward).

The whole story or indeed the entire progression of the pictures is almost without exception restful, portraying a game to be pondered and relished: only some of the photographs of modern times reflect the degree and extent of violence which has always been within the game but has only been captured by the action photographers of recent years. The purpose of all these pictures is to please; thus it has been argued by some that in the gouache, No. 17, of "A Landscape with Cricket Match", cricket itself is only incidental: but it is in truth the core of the picture.

The whole collection reflects the rise and richness of mid-nineteenth-century lithography, and it is to be lamented that, with the exceptions of Sicklemore's "View of Ireland's Royal Brighton Gardens" (No. 25) and Robert Cruikshank's "View of the Cricket at Darnall near Sheffield" (No. 6) there are no examples of aquatint which, during its boon period from 1775 to 1830, might well have taken cricket as a theme.

It is tempting to evaluate the artistic quality of the different contributions. In that case, while the single paintings must be excluded, the height of the popular field is that of the "Felix" lithographs, at their most handsome, hand-coloured in the fashion of the period.

They rake time, these pictures, recapturing periods as well as history but above all reflecting the fact that the game has altered completely without truly changing. The spectator at a Hambledon match could come to a modern Test Match and, while a few eyebrows might be raised if he hollered "Tich and turn", his understanding and his pleasure would be as great now as they were then. Perhaps he might find the over-rate strange, and the batsmen's perils disturbing, to one of his age. He would know it, though, for the game he knew.

This essay may well end with the words Sir Neville used to close his original "Discourse".

Never again shall we watch cricket set against a background of green trees, haystacks, barns, and a landscape of peace and plenty, remote from a world too busy getting and spending. That is one reason why the prints in this book are jealously worth preserving, a refreshment to the eye and mind, constantly renewing our love of 'The Noble Game'.

 PLATES

1

AN EXACT REPRESENTATION OF THE GAME OF CRICKET

Copper engraving by H. Roberts from a drawing made after the Life by L. P. Boitard. Published in 1743 by John Bowles at No. 13 in Cornhill
10¼in × 16in (26cm × 40·5cm)

"Inscribed to all Gentlemen Lovers of that Diversion"

Louis Peter Boitard (fl. 1750, d. 1758 or 1760) was born, and first studied art, in France. He came to England with his father and made a number of engravings from the work of the popular artists of the time, including Canaletto. His original work consisted largely of vignettes, portraits, designs, and illustrations.

This engraving is of no outstanding artistic merit, but it was considered sufficiently instructive to be engraved more than once, in one instance showing the cricket bat less curved than here. Boitard's original oil painting and preliminary sketch are at Lord's, while a similar oil painting is in the Tate Gallery, London.

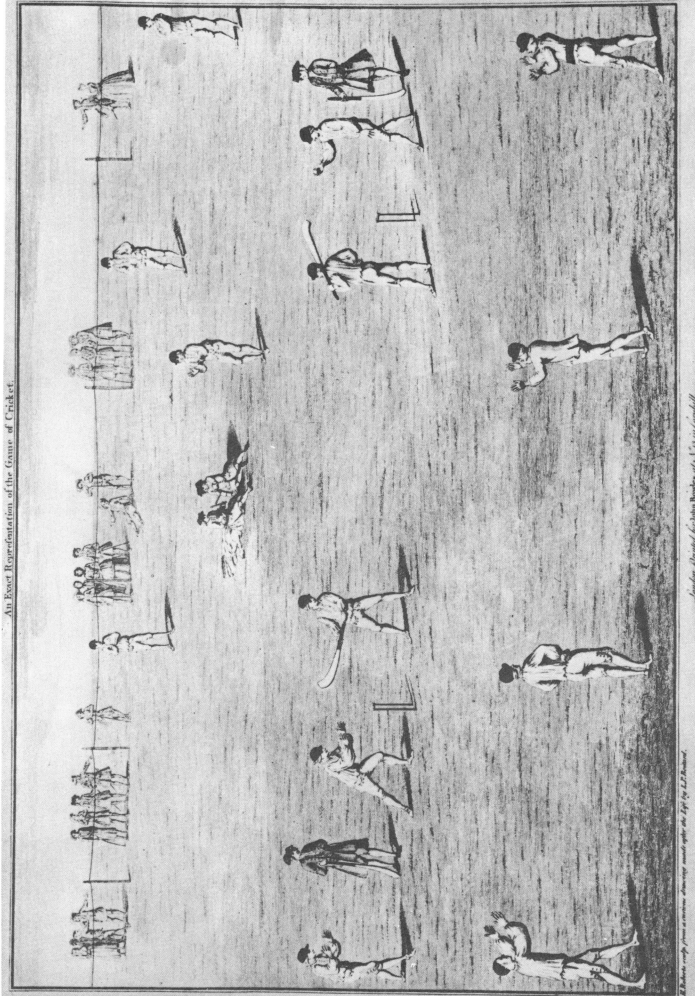

An Exact Representation of the Game of Cricket.

London Printed for John Bowles, at N 13 in Cornhill.

2

PAGE FROM GEORGE SHEPHEARD'S SKETCH BOOK, c.1790

7¾in × 9¾in (19·5cm × 25cm)

This is perhaps the most historically important, and unique, of all cricket pictures. It is the only pictorial representation of three of the Hambledon cricketers established in cricket history by their descriptions in Nyren's *The Cricketers of My Time*. It is remarkable that the drawings should have survived at all, for George Shepheard (1770–1842) was not an artist of any importance: little is known of him except that he occasionally played cricket for Surrey. One day he must have attended a match and jotted these sketches which surprisingly endured until they were acquired by the MCC at the beginning of this century.

The figures are, top row, left to right: Unknown; Thomas Lord (1752–1832) founder of Lord's Cricket Ground; Unknown; David Harris, of Hambledon, accepted as the finest bowler of the eighteenth century. Middle row: Tom Walker, the classic stonewaller of Hambledon; William—"Silver Billy"—Beldham, the supreme batsman of the age; a batsman said by E. V. Lucas to be George Shepheard himself; Thomas Lord. Bottom row: Colonel the Honourable Charles Lennox (1764–1819), fourth Duke of Richmond, who fought a duel with the Duke of York—he played in major matches for his patronage rather than his ability; Captain (later General) the Honourable Edward Bligh (1769–1840), also a more distinguished patron than player; Lord Frederick Beauclerk (1773–1850), Vicar of St Albans, descended from Charles II and Nell Gwynne, the finest amateur cricketer of his day, autocrat, and eventually President of the MCC; the Honourable Henry Tufton, a hard-hitting batsman as well as patron. The page is at Lord's.

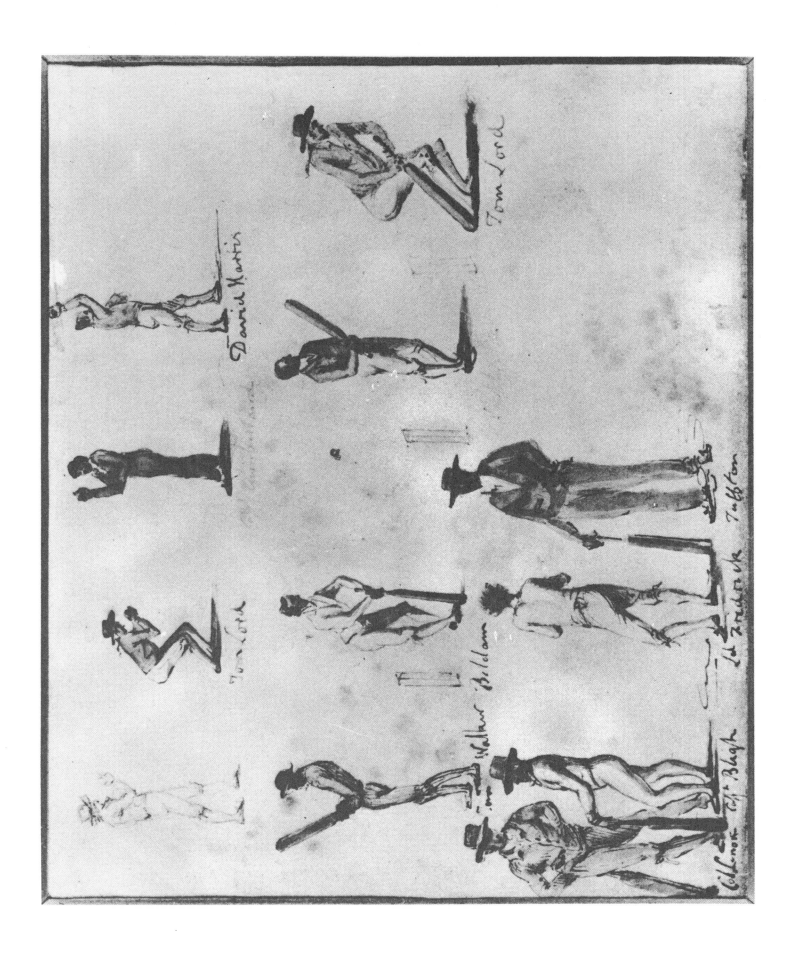

3

SCORECARD

9⅞in × 7⅛in (25cm × 18cm)

"A List of the Gentlemen Cricketers who played on Sevenoaks
Vine, July 3 & 4, 1782; for A Thousand Guineas. His Grace the
Duke of Dorset &c. against All England."

The headpiece is a variant on Hayman's *Marylebone Fields* (see Plates 19 and
24). The cricket world of a few years later would have been surprised to
see the leading professionals described as "Gentlemen Cricketers", but
it is, in fact, a match between the best professional players of the day, and
Scores and Biographies calls it Hambledon Club (here called England) v. Kent
with Bedster and Lumpy. This is an unusually early "running" scorecard:
it shows the state of the game after the second day's play: on the third,
Bullen and Hosmer (both misspelt here) made the few runs still needed and
Kent—"The Duke's Men"—won by four wickets.

A LIST of the GENTLEMEN CRICKETERS,

Who Played on SEVENOAKS VINE, JULY 3 & 4, 1782;

For A THOUSAND GUINEAS.

His Grace the DUKE of DORSET &c. against All ENGLAND.

With the STATE of the GAME.

The Duke's Men	First	Innings	Second		ENGLAND	First	Innings	Second
Mr. Brazier — -	1	B. Harris	0	C. Field	Mr. Small — — -	2	C. Book.	15	C. Bowr
Mr. Lumpy — -	17	B. Curry			Mr. Vick — — -	7	C. Bullin	0	C. Aylw
Mr. Bowra — —	4	B. Harri	48	C. Lear	Mr. N. Man — -	6	B. Lump	13	C. Bullin
Mr. Bedster — —	25	C. Harri	12	C. Curry	Mr. Curry — — -	8	C. Cliffor	6	B. Cliffor
Mr. Booker — —	29				Mr. Field - — —	16		6	B. Cliffo
Mr. Clifford — -	0	C. Taylo	15	B. Man	Mr. Lear — — -	1	C. Bowr	25	C. Ofme
Mr. Aylward - —	3	C. Franc	17	Run out	Mr. Taylor — —	0	C. Book	6	C. Book
Mr. Bulling — —	5	C. Franc	5		Mr. Hall — — -	4	B. Cliffor	2	
Mr. Ring — - —	3	C. Small	2	B. Man	Mr. Frances — -	10	B. Lump	15	B. Lump
Mr. Ofmer — —	6	C. Hall	9		Mr. Harris — —	27	C. Aylw	1	C. Bullin
Mr. Pattenden —	7	B. Man			Mr. Suter - — —	5	C. Bullin	48	B. Cliffor
Bye Runs —	2				Bye Runs —	1		3	
Total	102					87		140	

7 Oaks Printed

4

CRICKET AS PLAYED IN THE ARTILLERY GROUND, FINSBURY

Copper engraving by Benoist after Hayman. Published April 4th, 1743
10¼in × 13¾in (26cm × 35cm)

This is one of several engravings from the painting by Francis Hayman (see note to Plate 19) said to have been made when he and Hogarth were commissioned to provide the decor for Vauxhall Gardens (about 1738). The wicket-keeper is traditionally said to be a portrait of Hogarth. This primitive cricketing scene continued to be engraved, with slight variations, for many years.

The first major cricket match of which a full score survives (Kent v. All England, 1744) was played on this ground, which still exists in City Road, E.C.1, as the ground of the H.A.C.

CRICKET.

Serious, whom Nature has for this design'd
In the soft Charms of Ease no joy can find.

5

GRAND CRICKET MATCH
played in Lord's ground Mary-le-bone, on June 20th and following day
between the Earls of Winchelsea and Darnley for 1000 guineas.

*Copper engraving by Cook. Published July 1st, 1793, by I. Wheble, Warwick
Square, London*
3½in × 5¼in (9cm × 13·5cm)

This was the frontispiece to the June issue, 1793, of *The Sporting Magazine*;
it was accompanied by a printing of the laws of cricket. Neither engraving
nor laws are fully correct: the text mentions neither lbw nor the third
stump, and the picture does not show the latter.

The match, played between Lord Winchelsea's MCC team with three
Hambledon players (Beldham, Walker, and Wells) given, and Lord
Darnley's Kent team, was won by Lord Winchelsea's side.

This print, once barely considered, has lately become rare.

GRAND CRICKET MATCH, played in Lords Ground Mary-le-bone, on June 20.

following day between the EARLS of WINCHELSEA & DARNLEY for 1000 Guineas.

Published July 1, 1793, by I. Wallis, Warwick Square London.

6

NORTH EAST VIEW OF THE CRICKET GROUNDS AT DARNALL NEAR SHEFFIELD, YORKSHIRE

Sepia aquatint by Robert Cruikshank, "the landscape sketched by R. Thompson Esq."

6⅞in × 11in (17·5cm × 28cm)

Robert Isaac Cruikshank (1789–1856) had not the great gifts of his brother, George, but he was held in some esteem as both illustrator and etcher in an age of intense competition in those fields. He illustrated Westmacott's *The London Spy*, *Lessons of Thrift*, and *The Wit's Almanack*, and, in collaboration with his brother, Pierce Egan's *Life in London*.

It is indicative of the importance of Darnall Cricket Ground that it should be the subject of a plate by a fashionable London artist: indeed, the authoritative *Bell's Life* described it as "second to none" among English cricket grounds. That shown in the picture was the second at Darnall: the first was opened, by a Mr Steer, in 1821, but in the following year the stand collapsed and two spectators were killed. Mr Steer at once set about making a larger ground near by: it was ready for play in 1824. The artificial terrace provided seating for 8000 spectators and the ground was at first successful. Under the managership of W. H. Woolhouse it put on All England v. Twenty-two of Yorkshire in 1825 and, two years afterwards, the first of the historic "Experimental" matches, Sussex v. All England, which resulted in the change in the laws to permit bowling from the height of the shoulder (see note to Plate 52). All at once, however, for the simplest of socio-economic reasons, the ground failed. Darnall was three miles from the centre of Sheffield, the Hyde Park Ground only a mile and a half. Hyde Park became the centre of Sheffield and Yorkshire cricket and no great matches were played at Darnall after 1829.

NORTH EAST VIEW of the CRICKET GROUNDS at DARNALL, near SHEFFIELD, YORKSHIRE.

7

THE CUT

Lithograph, drawn from the Life & on Stone by G. F. Watts. Published by S. Knights, Sweetings Alley: printed by W. Sharp, 20 Gerrard St, Soho, London
11⅝in × 9½in (29·5cm × 24cm)

"Dedicated, with permission, to William Ward, Esqre by N. Felix"

G. F. Watts (see note to Plate 48) was only twenty when he made the five lithographs of cricket strokes which include this and Plate 8. In 1894 he presented his original sketches for the series to the MCC, and they show a process of translation from a left-handed to a right-handed batsman. Felix (Nicholas Wanostrocht), his former schoolmaster, publisher of the plates, and a fine left-handed batsman (see notes to Plates 36, 37, 39, and 54) would seem the obvious model; and the point of the drawings lay in the mechanics of the stroke, not the features of the batsman.

The power in the hands, the life of the body-poise, and the whole impression of mobility indicate a gifted artist at work.

The original drawing is at Lord's.

THE CUT.

Dedicated with Permission to William Ward, Esq.

By

N Felix

Drawn from the Life & on Stone by G F Watts   Published by S Knights Sweetings Alley

London.

Printed by W Sharp, 20, Gerrard St. Soho.

8

LEG VOLLEY

Lithograph, drawn from the Life & on Stone by G. F. Watts. Published by
S. Knights, Sweetings Alley: printed by W. Sharp, 20 Gerrard St, Soho, London
11⅝in × 9⅞in (29·5cm × 25cm)

"Dedicated, with permission, to Herbert Jenner, Esqre by N. Felix"

This lithograph belongs in the same series as Plate 7 and vies with it in life and poised vitality.

For G. F. Watts see notes to Plates 7 and 48: for N. Felix (Nicholas Wanostrocht) see notes to Plates 36, 37, 39, and 54.

The original drawing is at Lord's.

LEG VOLLEY.

Dedicated with Permission to Herbert Jenner Esq.

By

Drawn from the Life & on Stone by G. F. Watts.   N. Felix   Published by S. Knights, Sweetings Alley.

London
Printed by W. Sharp, 20, Gerrard St. Soho.

9

CRICKET: A GRAND MATCH

Poster: printed by W. A. Wright, 9 & 10, Fulwood's Rents, Holborn, 1849
17in × 10⅞in (43cm × 27·5cm)

In such posters as this cricket adopted the method of the theatre to attract patronage. This match was not of importance (though two matches of Islington Albion in the same season are recorded in *Scores and Biographies*) but it probably attracted a fair attendance of local people who, because of the limitations of local transport, took their pleasures near home. The figures in the pictorial headpiece are based on popular cricketers of the day.

CRICKET.

A GRAND MATCH!

WILL BE PLAYED AT THE

COPENHAGEN CRICKET GROUND,

Islington,

ON THURSDAY, AUGUST 9, 1849,

BETWEEN ELEVEN GENTLEMEN OF THE

ISLINGTON ALLIANCE CLUB,

AND ELEVEN GENTLEMEN OF THE

WINDSOR & ETON

JUNIOR CLUB.

☞ WICKETS PITCHED AT HALF-PAST TEN O'CLOCK.

N.B. Good Stabling.

W. A. WRIGHT, Printer, 9 & 10, Fulwood's Rents, Holborn.

10

PORTRAITS OF ALFRED MYNN, ESQ^r and N. FELIX, ESQ^r

Lithograph, drawn on stone by C. Cousens. Printed by C. Graf: published by Messrs. Baily Brothers, Royal Exchange Buildings, Cornhill

10in × 8⅜in (25·5cm × 22cm)

"Taken just previous to their playing the return Single Wicket
Match for the Championship of England at Bromley, Kent,
Septr 29th 1846."

For many years Alfred Mynn (see note to Plate 48) was the Champion of England at single wicket. Felix (Nicholas Wanostrocht) (see notes to Plates 39 and 54) challenged him in 1846. The law of single wicket that runs could not be scored from strokes behind the wicket gave Felix, a slow bowler, slight chance against Mynn's speed. In their two matches Felix received 262 balls in the first and 256 in the second, Mynn 16 and 52: yet Mynn won by an innings and one run and, in the return, with his wicket in hand. The second match was played on the ground attached to the White Hart at Bromley.

This is above all a picture of two friends: Mynn and Felix played together for Kent and were the only two amateurs to appear regularly for the All-England Eleven in its great days. Felix once wrote of their relationship, "From the first moment of our introduction we chimed in together, and every time we met only cemented our friendship."

On the Stone by L Greaves

Printed by J Graf

Portraits
of
ALFRED MYNN, ESQ^R and MR FELIX, ESQ^R.
taken just previous to their playing the return
Single Wicket Match,
FOR THE
CHAMPIONSHIP of ENGLAND,
AT
BROMLEY, KENT,
Septr 29th 1846.

11

THE BATSMAN

Lithograph, drawn from the Life & on Stone by G. F. Watts. Published by S. Knights, Change Alley, Cornhill: printed by Standidge & Co.

10½in × 8in (26·5cm × 20·5cm)

"Portrait of Fuller Pilch. Dedicated to the lovers of the noble game by N. Felix."

This is the companion to Plate 48. For N. Felix (Nicholas Wanostrocht) see notes to Plates 37, 39, 48, and 54. For G. F. Watts see notes to Plates 7, 8, 37, and 48.

Fuller Pilch (1803–70), who played for Norfolk, Kent, the Players, and the All-England Eleven, was probably the finest batsman of the period between William Beldham and W. G. Grace. Over six feet tall, correct in style and sound in temperament, he employed the forward stroke effectively. At one period he was a useful slow round-arm bowler but, apart from his batting, his main achievement in cricket was the management and tactical direction which lifted Kent to their position of dominance in the 1840s.

THE BATSMAN!
PORTRAIT OF FULLER PILCH.

Dedicated to the lovers of the noble game
By
N. Felix

Drawn from the Life & on Stone by G.F. Watts   Published by A.Baigrie, Ocean Row

12

THE GRAND CRICKET MATCH
between the Twenty-two of Ballarat and the Eleven of All England played
on the 6th, 7th, and 8th of March 1862

Lithograph by H. Deutsch, Ballarat
5¾in × 8½in (14·5cm × 21·5cm)

This is probably the rarest of all cricket prints. A genuine local production and an authentic period piece, it is one of the few cricket pictures virtually unknown to British collectors of cricketana.

The advertisement hoardings add to the convincing quality of a picture which at first gives the impression of being crowded because the Ballarat Twenty-two are in the field.

This was the ninth match of H. H. Stephenson's England team of 1862—the first to tour Australia. It was left unfinished after the Twenty-two had scored 122 and 107 and England 155: S. Cosstock made thirty-one for Ballarat and, for England, Iddison took thirteen wickets and Caffyn ten.

13

SIR SPENCER PONSONBY-FANE

Pencil drawing by N. Felix [Nicholas Wanostrocht]
11¼in × 9¼in (28·5cm × 23·5cm)

Sir Spencer Cecil Brabazon Ponsonby-Fane, P.C., G.C.B. (originally Ponsonby; he adopted the name Fane upon inheriting Brympton from Lady Georgina Fane) (1824–1914) was Comptroller of the Lord Chamberlain's office: he brought from Paris the treaty which ended the Crimean War.

He was fifteen when, in 1839, he first played for the MCC, and he visited Lord's regularly until 1913. He was largely responsible for the foundation of the fine collection of cricketana at Lord's. Ponsonby-Fane several times declined the Presidency of the MCC but was a committee member, treasurer, and trustee of the club, one of the original Old Stagers of the Canterbury Week, and a founder of I Zingari. He played cricket, primarily as a batsman, for Surrey and the Gentlemen.

14

ENGLAND v. AUSTRALIA AT LORD'S

Photogravure after H. Barrable and R. Ponsonby Staples, 1887
24in × 40¾in (61cm × 103·5cm)

This is not a representation of any specific match but a composite picture, made up by the artists of men who played for England and Australia at the time, and notable persons who attended Lord's.

W. G. Grace is the batsman, W. W. Read the non-striker, F. R. Spofforth the bowler, and T. W. Garrett is fielding the ball on the extra-cover boundary. The medallions below the title are of eleven cricketers of each country; a key was issued identifying the players on the field and a number of the spectators who are sitting in the old "A" enclosure.

There is a second significance to the picture: the Prince (later King Edward VII) and Princess of Wales are walking round towards the stand where several ladies whose names had been linked by gossip with the Prince are averting their heads from him. In the right centre foreground, to the right of the pillar, is Lily Langtry.

15

EIGHT DRAWINGS FROM "A CENTURY OF GRACE"

*Extracted from the hundred drawings of Dr W. G. Grace contributed by Harry
Furniss to "How's That" (Arrowsmith, Bristol: n.d.)*
Each approx. 4½in × 3½in (11·5cm × 9cm)

Harry Furniss (1854–1925) was a gifted caricaturist and illustrator: his
parliamentary illustrations for *Punch* and the *Daily News* were original and
amusing. Perhaps his most important work was his illustration of a com-
plete edition of Dickens (1910) but he was a flexible and perceptive all-
round draughtsman, as these sketches of W. G. Grace show (for Dr W. G.
Grace see note to Plate 60). The originals of many of the drawings in the
series are at Lord's.

16

DR W. G. GRACE

Drawing by Sir Max Beerbohm
12⅝in × 8in (32cm × 20·5cm)

"Portrait of dear old W. G.—to the left is the Grand Stand, to the
right, the funeral of one of his patients."

Sir Max Beerbohm (1872–1956), essayist and caricaturist, drew, generally, on artistic, literary, social, and political themes. This is one of his two known drawings of cricketers: the other, uncharacteristically and rather pointlessly savage, was of Ranjitsinhji. "Max" was one of the major figures of the Nineties and this drawing has eminence in both subject and artist.

The cheque bears the signature of Edward Lawson who was at that time (1895) editor of the *Daily Telegraph*. It was in 1895 that Grace made 1000 runs in May, and the *Daily Telegraph* organized a fund for him (contributions one shilling), which realized £10,000. (For Dr W. G. Grace see note to Plate 60.)

This drawing is at Lord's.

17

LANDSCAPE WITH CRICKET MATCH

Gouache: artist unknown, c.1750
18½in × 24⅞in (47cm × 63cm)

This sensitive landscape may be regarded as the most distinguished of all cricket pictures. The match is so small that it might be no more than incidental but the degree of artistic skill in composition is such that it becomes the focal point of the landscape.

It used to be attributed to Paul Sandby (1725–1809), drawing-master, landscape artist, and one of the first and best of the highly talented group of English topographical aquatinters of the period 1770–1830. Subsequent inquiries have cast doubt on that attribution. It has been suggested that it is the work of the even more eminent Richard Wilson (1714–82) whose work was influenced by Claude Lorraine and Gaspard Poussin and who was recognized, belatedly, as the first great English master of landscape painting.

A similar drawing was once in the possession of J. M. W. Turner who might be expected, on the evidence available, to have a considerable personal preference for Wilson as opposed to Sandby.

This painting is at Lord's.

18

HAMBLEDON: THE BAT AND BALL INN

Watercolour by Goddard Frederick Gale, 1879
9in × 12½in (23cm × 32cm)

The artist's note on this competent Victorian watercolour remarks that it shows the inn substantially still unchanged in appearance from a century earlier, when it was the headquarters of the Hambledon cricket club. Known as "The Hutt", it was kept by Richard Nyren, the captain and groundsman, and later by William Barber, one of the leading players. Apart from tile-hanging on the front it remained largely unchanged into this century. In 1907, E. V. Lucas found it "very squalid". There have since been considerable renovations and extensions, but the original core of the building can still be distinguished.

This painting is at Lord's.

19

A CRICKET MATCH IN MARY-LE-BONE FIELDS

Engraving, subsequently coloured, by C. Grignion after the painting by Francis Hayman. Published 1748
17¾in × 23⅝in (45cm × 60cm)

Francis Hayman (1708–76) was a contemporary and friend of Hogarth with whom he collaborated on the paintings for the alcoves at Vauxhall. His work is inferior but similar in style to Hogarth's. He was chiefly a painter of historical scenes but also executed some good portraits and illustrated several books. Two of his paintings of cricket scenes, including one called *The Royal Academy Club in Mary-le-bone Fields*—from which this engraving was made—are at Lord's. Variants of this engraving are shown in Plates 3 and 24.

20

MISS WICKET AND MISS TRIGGER

Coloured engraving "From the Original Picture by John Collet in the possession of Carrington Bowles." Printed for Carrington Bowles, No 69 in St Paul's Church Yard, London. Published as the Act directs, 1 Jan 1778
5⅜in × 8¼in (13·5cm × 11cm)

"Miss Trigger you see is an excellent shot
And forty five notches Miss Wicket's just got."

John Collet (1725–80) was a popular artist who painted in the style of Hogarth but without the same profundity, although the technical quality of his painting was high. He painted social scenes, often of low life, and his paintings were popular enough to be engraved by the best engravers and sold by the leading print-sellers of the time, such as Carrington Bowles. *Miss Wicket and Miss Trigger* has been frequently reproduced and its best form is probably as a coloured mezzotint.

Effeminacy

MISS WICKET and MISS TRIGGER.

Mifs TRIGGER you fee is an excellent SHOT, And forty five Notches Mifs WICKET's juſt got.

276 From the Original Picture by John Collet, in the poſſeſſion of Carington Bowles.

Printed for Carington Bowles, Nᵒ 69 in Sᵗ Pauls Church Yard, London. Publiſhed as the Act directs, 1 Jan. 1778.

21

STEDMAN'S HOUSE AND SCHOOL

Watercolour: artist unknown
11¾in × 16¼in (30cm × 41cm)

Cricket is only incidental, a part of a wider life, in this well-observed and warmly recorded school scene.

John Stedman (1744–97) had no connection with cricket and only the date, 1744, after his name on the frame—which appears contemporary with the painting—links it with him. He lived at Tiverton from no earlier than 1783 to 1797. Stedman was born in Holland, and served in the Scots Brigade, where he rose to the rank of lieutenant-colonel. He is best known for his book *Narrative of a Five Years' Expedition against the Revolted Negroes of Surinam*, in which he was much concerned with the social and natural history of the country, and which was illustrated with eighty of his drawings, engraved by William Blake and Bartolozzi.

This painting is at Lord's.

22

THOMAS HOPE

Oil painting by J. F. Sablet, 1792
24¼in × 19⅝in (61·5cm × 50cm)

Jean Francois Sablet (1751–1819) was a Swiss who worked in Rome, where he painted this portrait.

Thomas Hope (1769–1831) was the eldest son of John Hope, an English merchant in Amsterdam, and his Dutch wife. The son studied architecture, drew, wrote, and collected sculpture, pottery, and paintings. Like most of his family he left Holland upon the French occupation and settled in England where he enlarged his collection, made designs for furniture and costume, and wrote *Anastasius*, *An Historical Essay on Architecture*, and other studies.

Hope was on the Grand Tour when this portrait was made; Vesuvius is in the background. Hope is not known to have been a cricketer and probably, like many other men of his period, he was painted holding a bat which might as well, for the artist's purpose, have been a whip, a book, a glove, or a sword.

This highly accomplished painting was bought at Christie's in June 1968, the anonymous purchaser later allowing the MCC to buy it for the same price that he had paid at auction. The painting is at Lord's.

23

COUNTESS OF DERBY AND OTHER LADIES AT THE OAKS, SURREY, 1779

Watercolour by ''T. H.''
13½in × 28¼in (34cm × 71·5cm)

A pleasant example, typical of its period, in the genre established by Hogarth and employed outstandingly by Devis and Zoffany, which has been described as the ''conversation picture''.

This painting is at Lord's.

24

LAWS OF THE NOBLE GAME OF CRICKET

Copper engraving, coloured. London, published September 1st, 1785, by John Wallis, No 16 Ludgate Street, & L. Binns, Leeds
13¾in × 9⅝in (35cm × 24·5cm)

This is the headpiece to the first broadsheet edition of the laws. It is a pleasant version of Hayman's *Cricket in Marylebone Fields* (Plate 19) which was published thirty-seven years earlier but continued to appear, with some variations, on broadsheets of the laws, souvenir handkerchiefs, and popular representations of the game for another forty years.

Few pre-1786 printings of the laws were particularly reliable, but this, from "The Star and Garter", is better than most. It is the first to make mention of the third stump, when it adds to the third law: "N.B. It is lately settled to use three Stumps instead of two to each Wicket, the Bail the same length as above."

London Published September 1st 1785.

by John Wallis, No. 16 Ludgate Street & J. Binns Leeds

The LAWS of the NOBLE GAME of CRICKET,

as Established at the Star and Garter Pall-Mall by a Committee of Noblemen & Gentlemen

THE BALL.

Must not weigh less than five Ounces and a half, nor more than five Ounces and three Quarters.

It cannot be changed during the Game, but with Consent of both Parties.

THE BAT.

Must not exceed Four Inches and One Quarter in the Widest Part

THE STUMPS.

Must be Twenty two Inches, the Bail Six Inches long.

N.B. It is lately settled to use three Stumps instead of two to each Wicket, the Bail the same Length as above

THE BOWLING CREASE.

Must be parallel with the Stumps Three Feet in Length, with a Return Crease

THE POPPING CREASE.

Must be Three Feet Ten Inches from the Wickets; and the Wickets must be opposite to each other, at the Distance of Twenty-two Yards.

THE PARTY.

which goes from home,

Shall have the choice of the Innings and the pitching of the Wickets; which shall be pitched within Thirty Yards of a Centre fixed by the Adversaries.

When the Parties meet at a Third Place, the Bowlers shall toss up for the pitching of the First Wicket, and the Choice of going in

THE BOWLER.

Must deliver the Ball with one Foot behind the Bowling Crease, and within the Return Crease, and shall bowl four Balls before he changes Wickets, which he shall do but once in the same Innings.

He may order the Player at his Wicket, to stand on which Side of it he pleases.

THE STRIKER.

is out,

If the Bail is bowled off, or the Stump bowled out of the Ground : —

Or if the Ball, from a stroke over or under his Bat or upon his Hands (but not Wrists,) is held before it touches the Ground, though it be hugged to the Body of the Catcher

Or if in striking, both his Feet are over the Popping Crease, and his Wicket is put down, except his Bat is grounded within it.

Or if he runs out of his Ground to hinder a Catch.

Or if the Ball is struck up, and he wilfully strikes it again.

Or if in running a Notch, the Wicket is struck down by a Throw, or with the Ball in Hand before his Foot, Hand or Bat is grounded over the Popping Crease; but if the Bail is off, a Stump must be struck out of the Ground by the Ball.

Or if the Striker touches or takes up the Ball before it has lain still, unless at the Request of the Opposite Party.

Or if the Striker puts his Legs before the Wicket, with a Design to stop the Ball, and actually prevents the Ball from hitting the Wicket by it.

If the Players have crossed each other, he that runs for the Wicket that is put down is out; if they are not crossed, he that has left the Wicket that is put down is out.

When the Ball has been in the Bowlers or Wicket Keeper's Hands, the Strikers need not keep within their Ground, till the Umpire has called Play, but if the Player goes out of his Ground with an Intent to run before the Ball is delivered the Bowler may put him out.

When the Ball is struck up in the Running Ground between the Wickets, it is lawful for the Strikers to hinder its being catched; but they must neither strike at, nor touch the Ball with their Hands.

If the Ball is struck up, the Striker may guard his Wicket either with his Bat or his Body.

In Single Wicket Matches, if the Striker moves out of the Ground to strike at the Ball, he shall be allowed no Notch for such Stroke.

The WICKET KEEPER

Shall stand at a reasonable Distance behind the Wicket, and shall not move till the Ball is out of the Bowlers Hand, and shall not by any Noise incommode the Striker, and if his Hands, Knees, Foot or Head be over or before the Wicket, though the Ball touch it, it shall not be out.

THE UMPIRES.

Shall allow Two Minutes for each Man to come in, and Fifteen Minutes between each Innings; when the Umpire shall call Play, the Party refusing to play, shall lose the Match.

They are the sole Judges of fair and unfair Play, and all Disputes shall be determined by them.

When a Striker is hurt, they are to allow another to come in, and the Person hurt shall have his Hands in any Part of that Innings.

They are not to order a Player out, unless appealed to by the Adversaries. — But if the Bowler's Foot is not behind the Bowling Crease, & within the Return Crease, when he delivers the Ball, the Umpire unasked must call No Ball.

If the Strikers run a short Notch, the Umpire must call No Notch.

BETS.

If the Notches of one Player are laid against another, the Bet depends on both Innings, unless otherwise specified.

If one Party beats the other in one Innings, the Notches in the First Innings shall determine the Bet.

But if the other Party goes in a second Time, then the Bet must be determined by the Numbers on the Score.

THE END.

25

IRELAND'S ROYAL BRIGHTON GARDENS

*Coloured aquatint, drawn by H. Jones, engraved by Geo. Hunt. Published by
C. & R. Sickelmore, Stationers, 26 Kings Road, Brighton*
6½in × 11⅜in (16·5cm × 29cm)

This was originally issued, both plain and coloured, as Plate No. 4 of
Sickelmore's Select View of Brighton (c.1827) and then of *Sickelmore's
Descriptive Views of Brighton* (c.1830). The firm of Sickelmore published
a number of books about Brighton.

Joseph Ireland, formerly a linen-draper and haberdasher in Brighton,
opened his Gardens—designated "Royal" by George IV—in 1822 in
opposition to the Tivoli Strawberry Gardens. The scheme included a
bowling green, grotto, sitting-rooms, bar, billiard room, rackets and
fives courts, aviary, promenade-saloon, and maze, as well as a cricket
ground described at the time as "the best, perhaps, in the country".
Some major matches were played there (see note to Plate 38) but the
venture failed and the gardens were closed as a commercial concern in
1836. The ground remains as a civic recreation garden at the north end
of The Level.

26

RURAL SPORTS OR A CRICKET MATCH EXTRAORDINARY

Coloured engraving after Thomas Rowlandson (1756–1827)
9in × 13½in (22·5cm × 34·5cm)

The sub-title runs "On Wednesday October 3rd 1811 a Singular Cricket Match took place at Balls Pond, Newington. The Players on both sides were 22 Women, 11 Hampshire against 11 Surrey. The Match was made between two Amateur Noblemen of the respective Counties for 500 guineas each. The Performers in the Contest were all Ages and Sizes." The match was, in fact, played: it was won by the Hampshire women, who wore royal purple ribbons, while Surrey wore orange and blue. The engraving shows a two-stump wicket, although the third—middle—stump was introduced as early as 1776. The plate is unsigned but this is a typical Rowlandson composition: it is his only cricket print, although two water-colours of cricket scenes attributed to him were sold at auction in the 1960s.

27

GREENWICH v CHELSEA HOSPITAL PENSIONERS, 1825

Pencil and watercolour drawing by Henry Alken (1784–1851)
9½in × 14½in (24cm × 37cm)

Such freak matches as this between one-armed and one-legged players were frequently arranged in Georgian times for wagers and savage public amusement. This lively painting is the work of Henry Alken senior, one of a family of watercolour painters and engravers, who specialized in sporting and humorous subjects. He published his early work under the pseudonym ''Ben Tallyho''.

This painting is at Lord's.

28

THE CRICKET MATCH

Coloured aquatint after James Pollard. Published by Dean & Mundy,
September 1st, 1824
5½in × 15½in (14cm × 39·5cm)

James Pollard (1797–1867) was the son of Robert Pollard, a painter, engraver, and print-seller who specialized in sporting subjects. James made his chief reputation by his paintings and prints of coaching scenes, but he also produced racing, steeplechasing, fishing, and cricket pictures, characterized by the liveliness which is a feature of this one. He frequently made the engravings from his own paintings.

THE CRICKET MATCH.

Pub. Sept 7.1804 by Dean & Munday, Threadneedle Street

BOWL'D OUT OR THE K– –G & ALL ENGLAND AGAINST THE
BOROUGHMONGERS

Pen lithograph by C. J. Grant. Published by Tregar, Cheapside, April 25th, 1831
8¾in × 13¾in (22cm × 35cm)

This is a political cartoon based on William IV's agreement, on April
22nd, 1831, to the dissolution of Parliament after Grey's Government had
suffered a defeat in Committee on the first Reform Bill. The bowler is the
King, who knocks over the batsman, the Duke of Wellington, leader of
the Tories, with REFORM. The spectator shouting ''Foul, foul'' is Lord
Aberdeen, supporter of Wellington, and the figure on the extreme right is
the Duke of Cumberland. The fieldsmen are Sir Francis Burdett, Lord
Grey, Lord John Russell (saying ''That's what I call a purger''), and Lord
Brougham, all Whigs and supporters of electoral reform.

30

LORD'S CRICKET GROUND

Coloured engraving after C. Atkinson
7½in × 11⅞in (19cm × 30cm)

This view can be fairly accurately dated as after the building of the second pavilion (1826) and before that of the Church of Our Lady, Lisson Grove (1837) (see Plate 31).

The positions of the umpires—both at square leg—is interesting: so is the fact that each carries a bat (see H. S. Altham and E. W. Swanton, *A History of Cricket*, 1962: Vol. 1, p.27).

31

GRAND JUBILEE MATCH
played Monday, July 10th, 1837

Presentation silk handkerchief
17¼in × 19¼in (44cm × 49cm)

The Minutes of the MCC dated July 30th, 1836, record "The Marylebone Club having been established in the year 1787, it is resolved that a Jubilee Match shall take place at Lord's Ground on the second Monday in July, 1837, for the benefit of the Players, twenty-two of whom shall be chosen to perform on that day."

Two outstandingly strong teams were composed of the leading professionals and a single amateur, William Ward, a director of the Bank of England and M.P., who, in 1825, put up the money to buy the lease of Lord's and prevent it being developed as a building site. The match was over in two days: the South, who scored 60 and 70 for five wickets, beat the North, who scored 64 and 64 (with Box and Cobbett as 'given' men), by five wickets. Lillywhite took six wickets in the first innings of the North and eight in the second.

In the left distance are the stables and the original Tavern, to the left and right respectively of the Main Gate: the large building in the distance is the Church of Our Lady, Lisson Grove, and on the right is the second Pavilion, erected by William Ward after the previous one was burnt down in 1825.

The flag bears the name of J. H. Dark, first manager and then proprietor of Lord's Ground between 1832 and 1864.

Each member of the ground staff was given one of these commemorative handkerchiefs.

32

JOHN WISDEN

Coloured lithograph drawn and lithographed by John C. Anderson. Printed by Richard Black: published by John Corbet Anderson, 40 Church Road, De Beauvoir Square, England, April 1st, 1853, and by F. Lillywhite, 10 Princes Terrace, Caledonian Road, Islington
11in × 8in (28cm × 20cm)

John Corbet Anderson (1827–1907) had two separate reputations. The main interest of his life was antiquarian research; at the time of his death he was the oldest ticket-holder of the British Museum Reading Room and he was the author of *Croydon Church, Past and Present*. But his somewhat remarkable contribution to art and cricket was the series of well-observed watercolour portraits of cricketers made in the 1850s and published as lithographs which then enjoyed wide popularity and have since become esteemed collectors' items (see also Plates 34, 42, 50, and 52).

John Wisden (1826–84) played for Sussex and the All-England Eleven, and for some years, although quite small (five feet four and a half inches), was quite a fast round-arm bowler: in 1850, playing for the North against the South, he became the first bowler to clean bowl all ten wickets in an innings of a major match, and, according to *Scores and Biographies*, he turned "a yard from the off". Later he switched to slow lobs with some success, and throughout his career was an effective, correct batsman and a good slip field. At one period he was joint lessee, with George Parr, of a cricket ground at Leamington, and afterwards went into partnership with Frederick Lillywhite in a "cricket and cigar depôt" in Coventry Street, Leicester Square. He is best remembered, however, for founding *Wisden's Cricketers' Almanack* which first appeared in 1864 and remains the major work of reference on the game.

John C. Anderson del et lith.

Printed by Richard Black

WISDEN.

33

MATCH PLAYED AT CANTERBURY ON MONDAY, AUGUST 4th, 1845, BETWEEN KENT AND ALL ENGLAND

Coloured lithograph by W. Burgess. Published by H. Ward, Mercery Lane, Canterbury
11¼in × 19in (28·5cm × 48·5cm)

"To the President and Members of the Beverley and East Kent
Cricket Club this print is respectfully dedicated by their obedient
servant, Henry Ward."

This picture is of the chief match of the fourth "Grand Cricket Week" held at Canterbury. It was played on the ground of the East Kent (formerly Beverley) Club, on the Beverley Ground, beyond the Cavalry Barracks at Canterbury (the matches of the "Week" were not played at St Lawrence until 1847). The two elevens were outstandingly strong, for this was the period in which Kent had Pilch, Felix, the brothers Mynn, Adams, Dorrington, and Hillyer. Clarke took twelve Kent wickets in the match and England won by thirty-one runs.

Published by H. Ward, Mercery Lane, Canterbury.

To the President & Members of the Beverley and East Kent Cricket Club,
This Print, representing the Match played at Canterbury on Monday, August 4th 1823, between Kent & All Englands
is respectfully dedicated by their obedient Servant,

Henry Ward.

34

JOSEPH GUY OF NOTTINGHAM

Coloured lithograph drawn and lithographed by John C. Anderson. Printed by Richard Black: published by John Corbet Anderson, 40 Church Road, De Beauvoir Square, England, April 2nd, 1853, and by F. Lillywhite, 10 Princes Terrace, Caledonian Road, Islington
11½in × 8¼in (29cm × 21cm)

Joseph Guy (1814–73), who played for Nottinghamshire, the Players, and the All-England Eleven, was one of the three best batsmen of the 1840s, reliable against the best opposition and particularly effective against fast bowling: he also occasionally kept wicket. His style was so pleasing that a contemporary once said of him, "Joe Guy, all ease and elegance, fit to play before the Queen in Her Majesty's parlour".

For John Corbet Anderson see note to Plate 32.

JOSEPH GUY.

OF NOTTINGHAM.

35

VIEW OF THE CITY OF CHICHESTER

Coloured lithograph, drawn on stone by Henry Burn. Printed by M. & N. Hanhart, September 1852
11in × 20in (28cm × 51cm)

"To the subscribers of the Priory Park this View of the City of Chichester is most respectfully Dedicated by their Humble Servant the Artist."

This is a typical Victorian topographical lithograph. Priory Park ground at Chichester is still in use for cricket and until relatively recently Sussex played county matches there.

THIS VIEW OF THE CITY OF CHICHESTER.

TO THE SUBSCRIBERS

is most respectfully Dedicated by their humble Servant the Artist

36

LEG HALF VOLLEY

Coloured lithograph from "Felix on the Bat" by N. Felix [Nicholas Wanostrocht].
Printed by C. Graf: published by Baily Brothers, Cornhill, 1845
5½in × 5¾in (14cm × 14·5cm)

In this case there is an opportunity to compare the plate of the similar "Leg Volley" of Watts's series of 1837 (Plate 8) and, though the two are virtually identical in the depiction of position and action, this lacks the vitality of the earlier drawing. Though competent, this is undoubtedly the work of a lesser artist. (See also note to Plate 37.)

LEG HALF VOLLEY.

London. Baily Brothers, Cornhill.
Printed by C. Graf.

37

HOME BLOCK

Coloured lithograph from "Felix on the Bat" by N. Felix [Nicholas Wanostrocht].
Printed by C. Graf: published by Baily Brothers, Cornhill, 1845
5⅛in × 5¼in (13cm × 13·5cm)

There are three editions of *Felix on the Bat* all with different lithographic plates of batting strokes. This and Plate 36 are from the first edition. Felix (see notes to Plates 39 and 54) wrote that, for the illustrations to this edition, he "secured the services of Mr G. F. Watts and John Gilbert". Watts, who was a pupil at Felix's school, made a series of cricket lithographs (see Plates 7, 8, 11, and 48) which were published by Felix. This lithograph, however, is markedly inferior to the five by Watts made in 1837 and while one plate of attitudes may be by John Gilbert, it is possible that the colour plates were executed by Felix himself (see note to Plate 36).

HOME BLOCK.

London Baily, Brothers, Cornhill.

Printed by C. Graf.

38

A CRICKET MATCH BETWEEN SUSSEX AND KENT

Coloured lithograph. 'Pirated' and published by S. Lipschitz, 5 Commercial Street and 84 Brushfield Street, Spitalfields, from an engraving made by G. H. Phillips after portraits by W. Drummond and C. J. Basebe, and originally published by W. H. Mason, of Brighton, in 1849

18in × 23⅝in (45·5cm × 60cm)

Probably the best known of all cricket prints, it was announced in 1843 but only put out, after many modifications of plan, six years later. It was 'pirated' in Holland and by several English publishers but, for all its popularity, Mason, who envisaged and organized its publication, was almost bankrupted by the venture. This version is slightly compressed and less wide than the original. Mason's version was issued with a key plate naming seventy-two of the players and spectators. These twenty-two players never, in fact, all took part in the same match between Sussex and Kent but all of them played in the fixture between 1841 and 1846. The setting of the match is Ireland's Royal Brighton Gardens (see Plate 25). Below is a key showing the main characters represented in the lithograph.

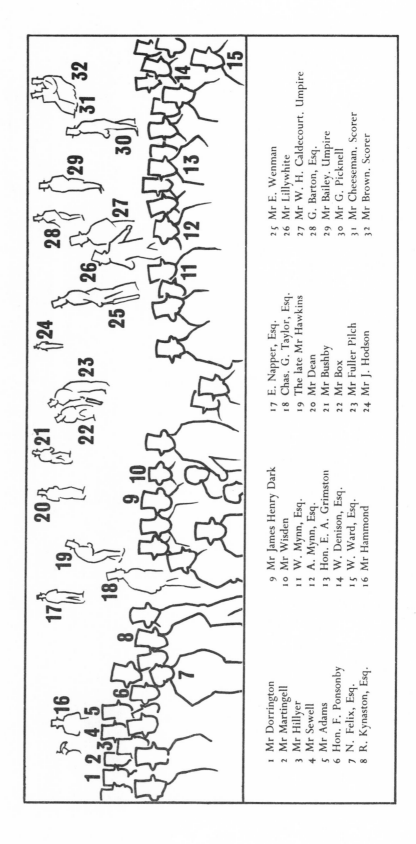

1 Mr Dorrington	9 Mr James Henry Dark	17 E. Napper, Esq.	25 Mr E. Wenman
2 Mr Martingell	10 Mr Wisden	18 Chas. G. Taylor, Esq.	26 Mr Lillywhite
3 Mr Hillyer	11 W. Mynn, Esq.	19 The late Mr Hawkins	27 Mr W. H. Caldecourt. Umpire
4 Mr Sewell	12 A. Mynn, Esq.	20 Mr Dean	28 G. Barton, Esq.
5 Mr Adams	13 Hon. E. A. Grimston	21 Mr Bushby	29 Mr Bailey. Umpire
6 Hon. F. Ponsonby	14 W. Denison, Esq.	22 Mr Box	30 Mr G. Picknell
7 N. Felix, Esq.	15 W. Ward, Esq.	23 Mr Fuller Pilch	31 Mr Cheeseman. Scorer
8 R. Kynaston, Esq.	16 Mr Hammond	24 Mr J. Hodson	32 Mr Brown. Scorer

39

THE ELEVEN OF ENGLAND SELECTED TO CONTEND IN THE
GREAT CRICKET MATCHES OF THE NORTH FOR THE YEAR 1847

Coloured lithograph by N. Ploszczynski from a watercolour drawing by N. Felix
[Nicholas Wanostrocht]. Published by Baily Bros, Cornhill, November 20th, 1847
18¾in × 23⅞in (47·5cm × 60·5cm)

Felix, an accomplished left-handed batsman for Kent, the Gentlemen, and
the All-England XI (see notes to Plate 54) was the owner and headmaster
of Alfred House Academy, Camberwell. His real name was Nicholas
Wanostrocht, but he played under the pseudonym of N. Felix at
first in case the parents of his pupils should disapprove of his association
with the not yet completely "respectable" game of cricket. He later
desired always to be known as Felix. He was an accomplished amateur
draughtsman, watercolourist, lithographer, and, later, painter in oils,
who published this and other lithographs (see Plates 7, 8, 10, 11, 13, 20,
36, 37, 40, 48, and 61).

This is the classic piece of portraiture of the players of Clarke's All-
England Eleven who had such a profound effect in creating and, by
example, teaching playing-standards in the mid-nineteenth century. The
names, from left to right are: Guy, Parr, Martingell, A. Mynn, W.
Denison [cricket writer], Dean, Clarke, Felix, Pell, Hillyer, William
Lillywhite, Dorrington, Pilch, Sewell.

THE ELEVEN OF ENGLAND.

40

HOW'S THAT!

Watercolour by N. Felix [Nicholas Wanostrocht], 1855
18⅞in × 15⅛in (48cm × 38·5cm)

Felix (see notes to Plates 39 and 54) played cricket for many years with Tom Box, of whom this is a portrait: in it Felix is at his best as a water-colour artist.

Thomas Box (1808–76) was the outstanding wicket-keeper of his time. He played for Sussex first in 1828 and finally in 1858: between 1832 and 1856 he took part in every match played by the county. He is seen here wearing gloves and pads, but in his early days he wore neither, and his bare-handed stumping of Sayers off the fast bowling of Brown was remembered as an unparalleled feat of dexterity.

This painting is at Lord's.

N Felix del. 1855

41

CRICKET MATCH AT CHRISTCHURCH, HAMPSHIRE

Oil painting, artist unknown, c.1850
21⅞in × 32⅝in (55·5cm × 83cm)

The fielding side is wearing the colours of the Bullingdon Club (see note to Plate 58), but since at this period most cricket teams wore coloured shirts, this is not necessarily significant. Indeed, Christchurch has no history of cricket of any importance and the match seems to have been no more than incidental in the mind of an artist attracted by a landscape dominated by the great Augustinian Priory Church, with the Castle ruins and the confluence of the Rivers Stour and Avon as other ingredients. The match is being played to the east of the town, between the north of Stanpit Marsh and Purewell.

This painting is at Lord's.

42

SKETCHES OF THE SURREY CRICKETERS
Sherman   Julius Caesar   Caffyn   Lockyer

Drawn and lithographed by John C. Anderson. Printed by R. Black, Red Lion Court, Fleet Street, London: published July 16th, 1852, by John Corbet Anderson, 40 Church Road, De Beauvoir Square, and by Frederick Lillywhite, 10 Prince's Terrace, Caledonian Road, Islington
11⅛in × 13⅜in (29·5cm × 34cm)

Thomas Sherman (1827–1911), of Surrey and the All-England Eleven and a founder of the "New All-England Eleven", was a fast bowler and impetuous batsman. After his playing career he coached at Harrow, Eton, Winchester, and Rugby.

Julius Caesar (1830–78) was an attacking batsman, alert fieldsman anywhere, and occasional bowler for Surrey, the Players, and the All-England Eleven.

William Caffyn (1828–1919) played for Surrey, the All-England Eleven, New South Wales, and the Players as an all-rounder, a brilliant stroke-making batsman, and accurate medium-pace bowler. In 1864, after his second tour to Australia, he remained there as a coach and is credited to a large degree with the development of the first-class game in that country. When he returned home in 1872 he could no longer keep a place in county cricket though he coached valuably.

Thomas Lockyer (1826–69), who followed Tom Box as the best wicket-keeper in the game, played for Surrey, the Players, and the United All-England. He was a reliable batsman and a conscientious team manager for his county and the "United".

For John Corbet Anderson see note to Plate 32.

The original painting is in the collection of Hal Cohen.

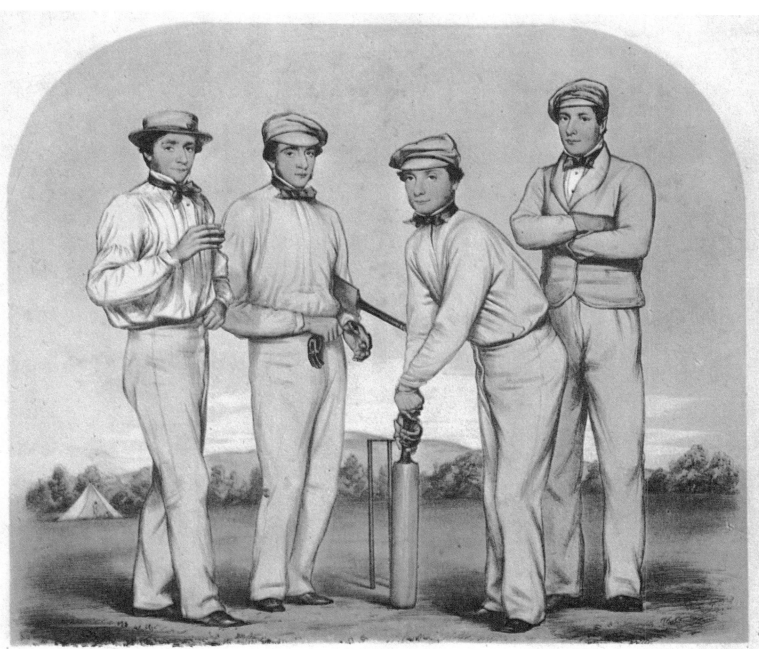

ASHERMAN.   JULIUS CÆSAR.   CAFFYN.   LOCKYER.

SKETCHES OF THE SURREY CRICKETERS.

43

ETON: GENERAL VIEW FROM THE PLAYING FIELDS

Tinted lithograph, drawn and lithographed by C. W. Radclyffe. Printed by Day and Haghe, lithographers to the Queen: published by T. Ingalton & Son, Eton,
1844
8in × 12½in (20cm × 32cm)

This was originally published as Plate No.8 of *Memorials of Eton College* by Charles W. Radclyffe, one of that artist's series of lithograph-illustrated books on English public schools. The view is of the College Field with the Cloisters and Chapel in the background, and the Wall in the middle right edge of the picture.

44

THE CRICKET GROUND, HARROW

Lithograph, drawn on stone by N. Whittock. Printed by C. Kellow, 11 High Holborn
4⅞in × 7in (11cm × 18cm)

Below the print there is a quotation from *Childish Recollections* by Lord Byron, who played cricket for Harrow against Eton in 1805:

> Yet when confinement's lingering hour was done,
> Our sports, our studies, and our souls were one;
> Together we impelled the flying ball,
>
>   *   *   *   *   *
>
> Together joined in cricket's manly toil.

Nathaniel Whittock was a well-known drawing-master and one of the earliest lithographers, a careful, if rarely imaginative, technician and illustrator.

45

THE TOWN AND UNIVERSITY OF CAMBRIDGE

Coloured lithograph, drawn by N. Felix, lithographed by N. Ploszczynski. Printed by M. & N. Hanhart: published by N. Felix, 1847
23⅞in × 37½in (60·5cm × 95cm)

Felix (Nicholas Wanostrocht) (see notes to Plates 39 and 54) painted this group in the same year as his *Eleven of All England* (Plate 39) but, although he has done his utmost to break up and yet balance the groupings, it is too crowded to produce the strong effect of the All-England Eleven print. Moreover, the players of these two teams are of less interest than those of the "A.E.": probably for these reasons not many copies of it seem to have been sold and it is by far the rarest of the English cricket lithographs of this period.

46

GEORGE PARR

Coloured lithograph by C. J. Basébe
10in × 6⅞in (25·5cm × 17·5cm)

C. J. Basebe exhibited at the Royal Academy between 1843 and 1879. A sensitive and capable artist, he was responsible for a number of cricket paintings (see Plate 38). In his watercolours he made effective use of Chinese white or, as here, the most delicate white wash.

George Parr (1826–91)—"the Lion of the North"—was, in succession to Fuller Pilch, the finest batsman in England, which then meant in the world. One of the greatest of all Nottinghamshire cricketers, he lived all his life in his native village of Radcliffe-on-Trent. He succeeded William Clarke as captain of both Nottinghamshire and the All-England Eleven: he also captained the strong England team which toured Australia in 1863–64, and played first-class cricket from 1844 to 1871.

47

VILLAGE CRICKET

Chromolithograph after an oil painting by John Ritchie
14⅛in × 19¾in (39cm × 50cm)

John Ritchie (fl. 1858–75) was a prolific and competent painter of warm, slightly sentimental landscapes much to Victorian taste. Of the many paintings of village cricket executed in this period, this is one of the more imaginative and least bleak. It has been suggested that it is of a match at Hambledon, but it might be almost any south-country village ground, and the church tower is not that of Hambledon.

The original painting is at Lord's.

48

THE BOWLER

Coloured lithograph, drawn by G. F. Watts, drawn on stone by Adam East.
Printed by Standidge & Co.: published by S. Knights, Change Alley, Cornhill
9⅞in × 8¾in (25cm × 22cm)

"Portrait of A. Mynn, Esq. Dedicated to the Lovers of the noble
Game by N. Felix" [Nicholas Wanostrocht].

G. F. Watts (1817–1904) produced five lithographs of batting strokes
which were published by Felix (Nicholas Wanostrocht) in 1837 (see
notes to Plates 7, 8, 11, 36, and 37). This portrait of Alfred Mynn is
one of a pair (the other, called "The Batsman", Plate 11, is of Fuller
Pilch): it was made later, though the precise date of publication is not
known. Felix must have been most happy to dedicate this portrait, for
both artist and subject were personally close to him.

Alfred Mynn (1807–61) was the popular, giant fast bowler of the mid-
nineteenth century. Six feet one inch tall and weighing between eighteen
and twenty stones, he played for Kent, the All-England Eleven, and the
Gentlemen. *Scores and Biographies* says of him "His delivery was noble,
walking majestically up to the crease ... his bowling was very fast and
ripping, round-armed and of a good length ... it was always considered one
of the sights at cricket to see Mynn advance and deliver the ball."

Mynn was also a capable, fast-scoring batsman, the most successful
single-wicket player of the period, and a man of honest and amiable
character; but he is remembered as the powerful, controlled bowler
whom the artist has caught so impressively in this portrait.

The original drawing is at Lord's.

THE BOWLER.

Portrait of A. Mynn, Esq.

Drawn from life by G.F. Watts.

On stone by Adam East.

Dedicated to the Lovers of the noble Game

By N. Felix.

Published by S. Knights, Change Alley, Cornhill

Printed by Standidge & C.º

49

THE CRICKET MATCH AT TONBRIDGE SCHOOL

Coloured lithograph by W. L. Walton after a painting by C. Tattershall Dodd.
Printed by Hullmandel & Walton, c.1851
19¼in × 31½in (49cm × 80cm)

This is perhaps the finest of the cricketing-topographical lithographs of the middle of the last century, sensitively balanced and pleasingly coloured.

Tonbridge School, founded in 1553, has a long tradition of cricket and has produced a remarkable number of players—most of them batsmen—for Kent. When this picture was painted there were 129 boys and Dr Welldon was headmaster. The cricket ground was laid in 1838, using soil from the near-by construction work on the South Eastern Railway.

50

THE UNITED ALL-ENGLAND ELEVEN

Coloured lithograph drawn and lithographed by John Corbet Anderson. Printed by Stannard and Dixon: published by F. Lillywhite, 10 Princes Terrace, Caledonian Road, Islington
17¼in × 23⅝in (44cm × 60cm)

The portraits, from left to right, are: Hunt, Wright, Adams, Mortlock, Lockyer, Wisden, F. Lillywhite, John Lillywhite, Dean, Caffyn, Grundy, Martingell, Sherman, and Sampson, and was the largest work of J. C. Anderson (see note to Plate 32).

The "United" was formed in 1852 as a result of the resentment felt by some members of the All-England Eleven at the tight-fistedness of William Clarke, who managed the "A.E." This print represents the team's main strength in the mid-1850s. Like the "All-England", the "United" toured England playing against local eighteens and twenty-twos, and when the feeling between the two elevens had grown less bitter than it was at the formation of the "United", the matches between the two elevens became the best cricket of the English season.

Frederick Lillywhite is sitting in his printing tent from which he issued scorecards and prepared match scores for the Press and his *Guide to Cricketers*.

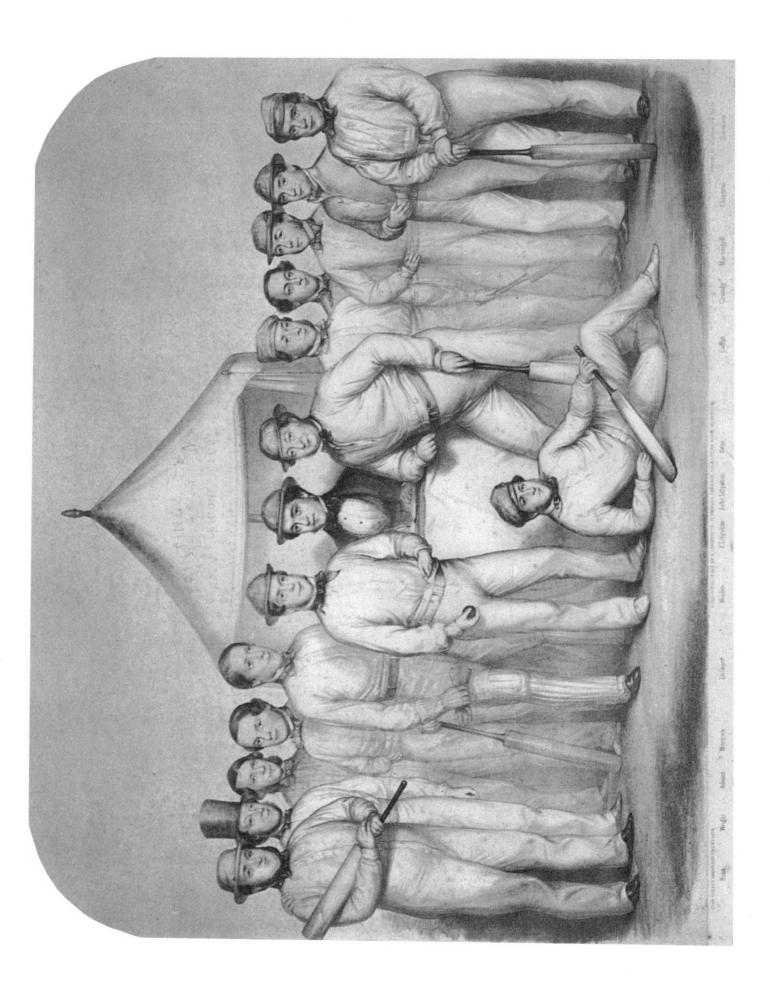

51

GRAND NATIONAL CRICKET MATCH

Lithograph, drawn on stone by S. T. Gill. Printed by Allan and Wigley: published by J. Fowles, 1857
10¾in × 18in (27cm × 46cm)

"Played at the Outer Domain, Sydney, January 14th, 15th, and 16th, 1857, by eleven players of New South Wales and eleven of Victoria, to Whom this Plate is respectfully dedicated by their obedient Servant, J. Fowles."

This is a view of the second intercolonial cricket match played in Australia. The first was between Victoria and New South Wales at Melbourne, the second was this return fixture.

Both matches were won by New South Wales. The Domain Ground at Sydney was used for intercolonial matches until 1869.

Drawn on Stone by S.T. Gill   Allen & Wigley Lith. Printers.

N.S.W. Players   **Victoria Players**

GRAND NATIONAL CRICKET MATCH.

PLAYED AT THE OUTER DOMAIN, SYDNEY, JAN'Y 12 & 16, 1857,

BY ELEVEN PLAYERS OF N.S.WALES & ELEVEN OF VICTORIA,

To whom this Plate is respectfully dedicated by their Obedient Servant

J. Fowles.

52

WILLIAM LILLYWHITE

Coloured lithograph by John Corbet Anderson. Printed by R. Black: published by F. Lillywhite and Wisden, 2 New Coventry Street, Leicester Square, London
11¼in × 7¼in (28·5cm × 18·5cm)

"William Lillywhite. Born June 13th 1792, as he appeared at Lord's Ground on July 25th 1853 in the Grand Match for his Benefit played between Sussex (with G. Parr) and England. This plate is respectfully Presented to the Subscribers."

(Frederick) William Lillywhite (1792–1854)—"The Nonpareil"—the greatest bowler of his time, played for Sussex, the Players, and the All-England Eleven. He was thirty before he first appeared in 'Great Matches' but he continued for over thirty years, and was a regular member of the All-England Eleven in its best period. He bowled slow right-arm with great guile and accuracy. He and Broadbridge employed round-arm bowling at a time when it was illegal and, through the 'Experimental Matches', brought about the change in the laws which allowed the bowler to deliver from the height of the shoulder.

The Lillywhite family—"Old Lilly's" sons and nephews—played a considerable part in Sussex and national cricket, the sale of cricket equipment, and the publication of various cricket annuals, books, and records.

John Corbet Anderson del. et lith.   Published by F. Lillywhite & Wisden, 2, New Coventry St. Leicester Sq. London.   Printed by R. Black

WILLIAM LILLYWHITE.

53

NORTHUMBERLAND CRICKET GROUND, NEWCASTLE UPON TYNE

Coloured lithograph by M. & M. W. Lambert, c. 1844
9⅝in × 14⅜in (24·5cm × 36·5cm)

This was the ground of the Northumberland Cricket Club which was purely a private club and not the county club. In 1839 it became the club's first private ground: its matches until then had been played on the Town Moor. It was then on the edge of the city, though its site is near the present centre, between St Mary's Place and Northumberland Road.

The club occupied it from 1839 until it was sold for building in 1881. Dame Allan's School (the present College of Commerce building) and St George's Drill Hall were built on the original playing area, while the City Baths stand on the site of the classically arched club house in the centre distance of the picture.

St Thomas's Church—architect, John Dobson—was once on the Tyne Bridge: it was re-erected on this site about 1820.

The Northumberland Club moved to Heaton but when, in 1897, the Northumberland County Club took over its present ground, previously the Constabulary Ground, at Jesmond within the city boundaries, the old Northumberland Club went into decline, many of its players joined other clubs, and it ceased to exist after 1899.

NORTHUMBERLAND CRICKET GROUND.

54

N. FELIX ESQRE

Coloured lithograph
13⅞in × 10in (35cm × 25·5cm)

''No 1 Series of Cricketers. Born at Camberwell in Surrey,
Octr 5th 1804''

This almost certainly is a self-portrait; Gerald Brodribb, the biographer of Felix, comments that his face always appears more handsome in his self-portraits than in the work of other artists. Felix (Nicholas Wanostrocht) (1804–76) was of Belgian extraction: a man of many talents, he was a writer, musician, painter, and the best amateur batsman of his time. He played for Kent and the All-England Eleven and was chosen regularly for the Gentlemen against the Players from 1831 until 1852. A left-handed batsman, he was renowned for the brilliance of his cutting; he also bowled lobs usefully.

Felix invented the 'Catapulta'—a bowling machine—and tubular batting gloves: he was the author of *Felix on the Bat*, an illustrated instructional book on batting, written with touches of period—punning—humour, and a pamphlet called *How to Play Clarke*.

55

KNOWLES HILL, NEWTON ABBOT, FROM THE SOUTH DEVON
CRICKET GROUND

Coloured lithograph by Newman & Co., 48 Watling Street, London. Published by
G. Daimond, Newton Abbot
5¾in × 9½in (14·5cm × 23cm)

Newman's firm also produced a book of lithographic views of Bournemouth in about 1850.

The South Devon Club, which still plays on the ground at Newton Abbot shown in this plate, was founded in 1851. According to the *Annals of the Teignbridge Cricket Club* (1888) Teignbridge (founded 1823) was the first permanent cricket club in Devonshire. Teignbridge are believed to have played at one period at Teigngrace, about two miles out of Newton Abbot—and a little farther from Teignbridge—and certainly their Treasurer lived at West Ogwell House, Newton Abbot. Their records show that they played a match with the South Devon Club in 1881. Before that, however, there seems to have been some overlapping of the two clubs and, later, amalgamation.

The South Devon has long been one of the strongest sides in a county where club cricket is enduringly healthy.

Published by G.Dsmond,Newton Abbot.

Lithographed by Newman & Cº 48,Watling Stʳ London.

Knowles Hill from the South Devon Cricket Ground.

56

THE FIRST INTERNATIONAL MATCH PLAYED BY THE ALL-ENGLAND ELEVEN AND XXII OF VICTORIA
Melbourne Cricket Ground, January 1st, 1864

Coloured lithograph published by Ch. Trodel, Melbourne Album Office, 1864
10⅜in × 14in (26cm × 35·5cm)

This is the classic print of Australian cricket, a view of the first match of the second English team to visit Australia. The team, captained by George Parr, included E. M. Grace and most of the leading professionals of the day. Lockyer of Surrey (see Plate 42) stumped six and caught five. At the end, England, who had needed 114 to win, were nine runs short with six wickets standing.

The match was played on 1st, 2nd, 4th, and 5th January, and the total attendance was 40,000.

The site is that of the ten acres of the Government paddock leased to the Melbourne Cricket Club in 1853 after a railway was built through its earlier ground, south of Yarra. The present Melbourne Cricket Ground— the "M.C.G."—stands in the same place and held the record for attendance at a single match (933,513 for Australia v. England, 1936–37) even before the extensions for the 1956 Olympic Games, planned to increase its capacity to 150,000. The ground is also used for Australian Rules football matches.

57

GRAND INTERCOLONIAL CRICKET MATCH, MELBOURNE, JANUARY 1, 1864

Woodcut, coloured, by Edward Gilks. Printed by J. M. Gerguson & J. Finnie
9½in × 15in (24cm × 38cm)

As a result of a dispute between Victoria and New South Wales after their match at Sydney in 1863, there was *no* intercolonial match at Melbourne in 1864. The match played at Melbourne on January 1st, 1864, was, of course, that between England and XXII of Victoria, the subject of Plate 56. Even if allowance is made for a different viewpoint, the difference between this scene and that of the Trodel is remarkable and, in the absence of evidence of publication date, one may wonder whether the word "Intercolonial" or the date "1864" is in error.

GRAND INTERCOLONIAL CRICKET MATCH, MELBOURNE, JANUARY 1, 1864.

58

CRICKET AT BULLINGDON ON A SUMMER'S AFTERNOON

Coloured lithograph. Published by Ryman, High Street, Oxford, c.1850
11in × 15½in (28cm × 38·5cm)

The cricket ground of the Bullingdon Club was at Bullingdon Green, to the north of the early Oxford University ground on Cowley Common. The club played MCC there on the first recorded occasion on June 15th, 1795. The University Match of 1843 (which Cambridge won by 54 runs) also took place on this ground. Subsequently William Lillywhite said it was the finest turf he had ever played on, but the outfield can hardly have been good, for the other main sport of the members was horse-racing.

59

RUGBY: NEW BIG SIDE—CRICKET

Coloured etching by F. Hunter from a painting by H. Jamyn Brooks, 1889
13⅞in × 19⅞in (35cm × 50·5cm)

Rugby School (founded 1567) is one of England's major public schools. *Tom Brown's Schooldays* and the beginning of Rugby football have made Bigside the best known of school playing-fields. Rugby is the last school still to play in coloured shirts (light blue). The most celebrated of the many fine Rugbeian cricketers is Sir Pelham Warner.

The original painting is at Lord's.

60

''CRICKET'

Colour lithograph by ''Spy'' (Sir Leslie Ward: 1851–1922). Published in ''Vanity Fair'' of June 9th, 1877
12¼in × 7¼in (31cm × 18·5cm)

This is a caricature of Dr W. G. Grace, No. CL in the *Vanity Fair* series ''Men of the Day''. Sir Leslie Ward worked for *Vanity Fair* from 1873 to 1909, and this drawing is markedly in his early style when there was a strong element of caricature in his work: his later studies are orthodox portraits of much care but less character.

Dr William Gilbert Grace (1848–1915) was the most important figure cricket has known. Over a long career (1865–1908) in first-class cricket, in which he played chiefly for Gloucestershire, the Gentlemen, MCC, London County, and England, he virtually created the modern techniques and strategies of cricket. Those who saw him play, even late in life, did not doubt that he was the finest of all batsmen, and certainly for many years he stood head and shoulders above all others. ''W.G.'' was the first cricketer to score a hundred centuries and only since the First World War has anyone surpassed his career total of 54,896 runs. He also took 2876 wickets, and for most of his life was automatically appointed captain of every team for which he played.

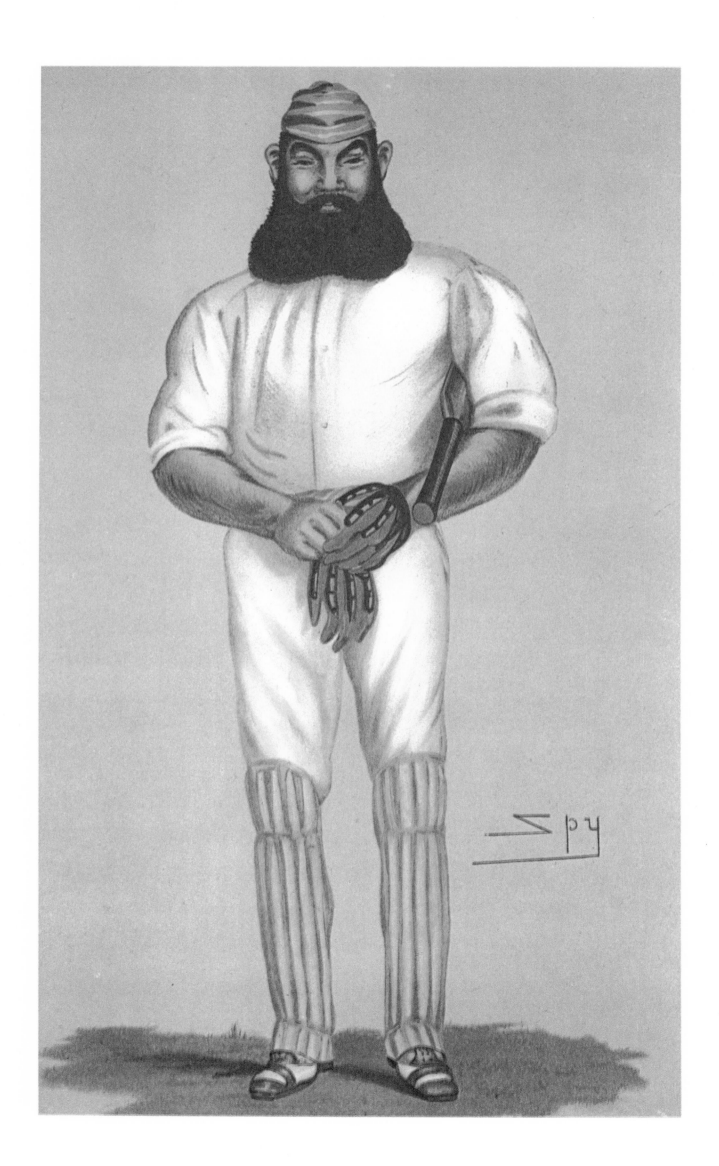

61

"THE DEMON BOWLER"

Colour lithograph by "Spy" (Sir Leslie Ward: 1851–1922). Published in "Vanity Fair" of July 13th, 1878
12¼in × 7¼in (31cm × 18·5cm)

This is a caricature of F. R. Spofforth, No. CLXXXIII in the *Vanity Fair* series "Men of the Day". Here again is a characteristically humorous example of the early drawing of "Spy" (see note to Plate 60).

Frederick Robert Spofforth (1853–1926) played for New South Wales, Victoria, Australia, and, briefly at the end of his career, Derbyshire. He bowled right-arm, employing a sharp break-back, at pace varied skilfully between medium and fast. In eighteen Test Matches against England between 1876 and 1886 he took ninety-four wickets.

At Melbourne in 1879, in the historic defeat of England at The Oval in 1882 (when he took fourteen wickets), and the two Sydney matches of 1885 his bowling was the match-winning factor.

The original painting is in the possession of J. Arlott.

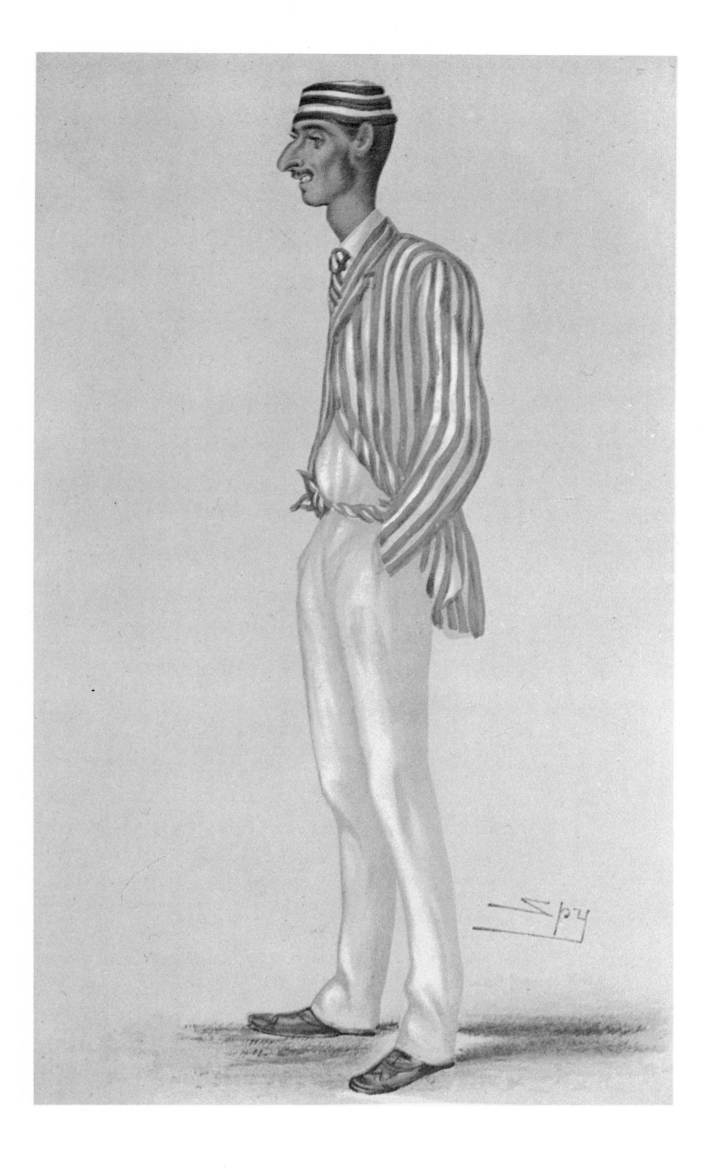

62

"THE CRICKETER"

Coloured lithograph. Song-cover, printed by J. & W. Pearman, 13 Castle Street, East: published by Weippert & Co. (late Simpson), 286 Regent Street, London
13⅜in × 8⅝in (34cm × 22cm)

The portraits are of Clarke, Pilch, and MacLagan (who sang the song on the stage), and the views are of Lord's and The Oval. This is as typical a mid-Victorian song-cover as the song—"Written and composed by W. J. Bullock"—is a typical popular ballad of the period:

> Then take the bat and the ball in hand,
> Let the umpire sing out "play"
> For cricket is a noble game
> And 'tis our toast today.

63

"ENGLISH CRICKET"

Colour lithograph by "Ape" (Carlo Pellegrini: 1839–89). Published in "Vanity Fair" of September 20th, 1884
12¼in × 7¼in (31cm × 18·5cm)

This is a caricature of the Hon. Alfred Lyttleton, No. CCCXIV in the *Vanity Fair* series "Men of the Day".

Carlo Pellegrini, an Italian from Capua, was one of the first and finest of the *Vanity Fair* cartoonists: some of his best studies were of politicians, notably Gladstone and Disraeli. He signed his early work "Singe" but it was as "Ape" that he established his high reputation. He executed a few portraits in oils and was himself painted by Degas.

The Hon. Alfred Lyttleton, K.C. (1857–1913) played most of his first-class cricket for Cambridge University, Middlesex, MCC, the Gentlemen, and England. He was England's wicket-keeper in the Test Match of 1880, 1882, and two of the three in 1884. As a batsman he was known as a fast scorer and primarily a forward player. In 1884 at The Oval, when Australia passed 500 with only six wickets down, Lyttleton took off his pads and, bowling lobs, took four for nineteen. He was a barrister and became an M.P. and Colonial Secretary (1902–5). A double international—he played Association football for England—he was also considered the best amateur tennis player of his time.

The original painting is in the collection of Hal Cohen.

64

JUNE

Coloured woodcut from "An Almanac of Twelve Sports" by William Nicholson (words by Rudyard Kipling). Published by William Heinemann, London, 1898
$7\frac{7}{8}$in × $7\frac{7}{8}$in (20cm × 20cm)

Sir William Newzam Prior Nicholson (1872–1949) was a versatile artist. The *Almanac*, of which this was the sixth plate, was one of a series of wood-cut illustrated books that he published. His best work was probably in portraiture, but he collaborated with James Pryde in the "Beggarstaff" posters, designed stage scenery and costumes, and was responsible for at least one fine conversation piece.

The batsman in this woodcut is presumably Alfred Mynn (see notes to Plates 10 and 48).